THE ROCKS AND SCENERY OF GUERNSEY

by

Mick de Pomerai and Andy Robinson

Illustrated by Nicola Tomlins

1994
Reprinted 2000 and 2008
published by
La Société Guernesiaise
Candie Gardens, St. Peter Port, Guernsey, GY1 1UG

TABLE OF CONTENTS

THE ROCKS AND SCENERY OF GUERNSEY

Introduction

Many holidaymakers who come to Guernsey delight in the variety of its coastline and scenery, the impressive cliffs of the south coast, the wide sandy bays of the west, the heathland of L'Ancresse in the north and the picturesque country valleys into which one unexpectedly descends having taken yet another wrong turning! Similarly, the contrasting colours of the cliffs around the coastline and the variety of attractive beach pebbles to be found must have intrigued many a visitor to our shores.

This booklet has been written in response to such interest by members of the Geological Section of La Société Guernesiaise, a group of largely amateur geologists, with the aim of explaining the story of Guernsey's rocks and scenery to the interested layperson. We have tried, therefore, to avoid too many technical terms. Those which we have used in the first chapter are explained in the appendix and glossary at the end of the book. We have based the book on a series of excursions to places of particular geological or scenic interest around the island, which are also reasonably easy of access.

A short bibliography of other, more detailed geological publications relating to Guernsey is included for those who wish to find out more. Many of these are available from the Guernsey Museum and Art Gallery, St. Peter Port, or from La Société Guernesiaise.

This booklet was first printed in 1994. With this reprint, the opportunity has been taken to make a number of minor revisions to the original text and also to make a small extension to Itinerary 7 - Herm Island.

ACKNOWLEDGEMENTS

The authors would like to thank their long-suffering wives who have had to endure sudden and protracted disappearances of their husbands in gathering information for this publication. Thanks also go to Alan Howell of the Guernsey Museum and Art Gallery for his advice and drawing attention to certain technical details that required amending. We are also indebted to Griff Caldwell of La Société Guernesiaise for his support and drive in organising and pursuing the publication of this work. Lastly, we wish to express our thanks to Carolyn Harbour for typing the text and patiently coping with the many alterations, and to Peter Hancock for his help in producing the map.

THE GEOLOGICAL HISTORY OF GUERNSEY

The island of Guernsey, though small in area (some 25 square miles) boasts an extensive geological history dating back more than 2,500 million years to some of the oldest rocks found anywhere in Europe.

In terms of both its scenery and the underlying geology, Guernsey can broadly be divided into two areas. The southern part of the island is formed largely of ancient metamorphic rocks, known as the Icart and Perelle gneisses, which are thought to be around 1,000 to 2,000 million years old. These rocks, forms an elevated plateau, dissected by several deep, often wooded, and very attractive valleys such as the Talbot, St. Peters and Petit Bôt valleys. The plateau is flanked to the south and east by spectacular cliffs which are well-served by a network of paths. To the west, the descent to sea level is somewhat more gentle, an ancient cliffline (now a steep, wooded slope) descends to a series of low-lying "marais" which form a narrow coastal plain.

The northern part of the island is formed of rather younger igneous rocks, such as granite, diorite and gabbro, which are around four to five hundred million years old. The landscape of northern Guernsey is generally more low-lying, though there are several small hills ("hougues") where harder rocks have resisted erosion more effectively. The higher ground of the Vale Parish between Bordeaux and L'Ancresse was, until the eighteenth century, a separate island linked to Guernsey by St. Sampson's Bridge.

Around Guernsey's coastline are found numerous deposits of material formed during the last few thousand years. These include rubbly "head" dating from the last Ice Age, pebbly raised beach deposits formed during intervals of higher sea-level, and submerged peat beds (suggesting periods of lower sea level) which are occasionally uncovered by storms.

Fossils are, regrettably, rare in Guernsey, although the remains of trees and mammals (also flint implements) have been found in the peat and raised beach deposits. Flint pebbles washed up on the beaches may occasionally contain fossil remains of sponges and sea-urchins.

The nature of our landscape reflects both the underlying geology and the influence of varying sea levels and climatic conditions over the last 10 million years or so (the Tertiary and Quaternary Eras). These are described in the following pages.

The Southern Metamorphic Region

The plateau of southern Guernsey is composed largely of the Icart and Perelle Gneisses, both metamorphic rocks. The Icart Gneiss (pronounced ee-car-nice) forms much of the south coast cliffs of the island, and is an easily recognised pale grey, coarse-grained rock containing large pinkish feldspar crystals around which are deformed masses of quartz, mica, and hornblende, giving the whole rock a rather "squashed" appearance. The Icart Gneiss is now generally believed to have originated as an intrusion of granite around 2,000 to 2,500 million years ago, into even older rocks whose remnants can still be discerned as "rafts" or xenoliths of schist such as the Jerbourg Metasediment (see Itinerary 2). These schists have a finer, flaky texture and contain minerals and structures which suggest their origin as silty sediments formed on a sea-floor perhaps 2,600 million years (or more) ago.

The Perelle Gneiss also originated as an igneous rock, probably a diorite intrusion. It is much darker in colour, comprising mainly hornblende and feldspar, again showing evidence of metamorphism under pressure by the alignment of its minerals. The age of the Perelle Gneiss, and the date(s) of metamorphism of both the gneiss groups is somewhat uncertain, but perhaps around 1,000 million years ago.

The time-scale involved in the formation of such rocks is scarcely imaginable. The Jerbourg sediments must have been deeply buried beneath overlying layers as the Earth's crust slowly subsided over millions of years. They were then compressed, deformed and intruded by granite magma and finally heated and deformed still further to form schist and gneiss. The process of slow uplift and erosion of the overlying rocks has been equally gradual, for it has taken another billion years for these rocks to become exposed at the Earth's surface.

All of these older rocks in the Channel Islands and in the nearby Cotentin and Brittany peninsulas are referred to as being of "Pentevrian" age, a term rather loosely used to cover a series of igneous and metamorphic events which took place over a very long period indeed.

At Pleinmont, in the far west of the island, is a small region of rather dull, brownish-grey, fine-grained rock known as the Pleinmont Metasediment (though its sedimentary origin is barely discernible). This belongs to the "Brioverian" sequence, represented in Jersey by a thick shale formation and by extensive sedimentary sequences in north-west France. The Jersey Shale formation contains the only fossil remains in the Channel Islands; though these are only worm burrows, they clearly testify to a period of perhaps 300 million years during which the sea covered much of the Channel Islands region. Towards the end of the period, around 700 million years ago, volcanic activity in Jersey and northern France heralded the beginning of the Cadomian Orogeny (see below) and the emplacement of the igneous complex which forms the northern part of Guernsey, along with Herm and Jethou.

The Northern Igneous Complex

The northern part of Guernsey (along with the L'Erée area in the west) comprises a series of igneous intrusions of granites, granodiorites, diorites and gabbro.

In order to make any sense of this variety, it may help to explain firstly the setting of all this intense activity.

Whilst little is known about the earth movements associated with the formation and deformation of the Pentevrian metamorphic rocks, we do know a great deal more about the events which took place following the close of the Brioverian around 700 million years ago. The events of the ensuing 200 million years belong to what geologists term the Cadomian Orogenic cycle. (Cadomian from the Norman name of Caen and orogenic meaning "earth-building").

It seems that the marine basin in which the Brioverian sediments were laid down began to close as two plates of the Earth's crust moved together, with one plate being forced down beneath the other as is happening today, for example, beneath eastern Japan, or western South America. (See Appendix)

When one crustal plate is forced down beneath another, it is not surprising that immense stresses are built up, resulting in earthquakes and deformation (folding and faulting) of the crustal rocks. Water, released as the down-going slab is heated up, enables some of the crustal and mantle rocks to melt and form bodies of magma, which then rise upward toward the surface. Such magma bodies, however, do not necessarily reach the surface, and may often cool and crystallise slowly at depths of several kilometres. Such is the case with the rocks of northern Guernsey. One can imagine, however, that at the time these intrusions were emplaced, there may well have been violent volcanic eruptions at the surface. Although these volcanoes have long since been removed by erosion, evidence of their former existence is suggested by slightly older (late Brioverian) volcanic rocks in Jersey.

The earliest phase of Cadomian activity in Guernsey is represented by the intrusion of the L'Erée granite, dated at around 650 million years ago. Continuing compression and deformation is indicated by the later conversion of parts of this granite to a gneiss, along with folding and brecciation (breaking up) of the Pleinmont Metasediment immediately adjacent to the granite.

The next phase of magma intrusion is represented by the St. Peter Port Gabbro, dated around 500-550 million years. This dark grey rock, with its characteristic large hornblende crystals, forms the foreshore between Castle Cornet and Vale Castle and is a common building stone used in the town. It has many interesting features, not least of which is the repeated layering of hornblende and feldspar crystals which has been the subject of some controversy in recent years (see Itinerary 5).

The last phase of intrusive activity, around 500 million years ago, began with the formation of the grey Bordeaux Diorite, perhaps through mixing of granitic and gabbroic magmas at great depth to form this intermediate rock type. Over the next few million years, the Bordeaux Diorite was followed in turn by the intrusion of the Cobo Granite - its vivid orangey-pink colour clearly recognisable in the rocks of Cobo Bay - and then finally by the pale grey L'Ancresse Granodiorite. It seems that each of these intrusions had barely cooled to a solid state when the next arrived, so that their contacts show some very odd relationships - such as the extraordinary "granite pipes" seen invading through dark "meladiorite" at Beaucette Marina (see Itinerary 5).

By about 490 million years ago, the Cadomian Orogeny came to an end with the last phase of minor deformation and formation of minor intrusions in the north of the island. The whole region had now been considerably uplifted, and was undergoing active erosion; the Rozel Conglomerate of north-east Jersey, and the Alderney Sandstone (along with similar deposits in north-west France) date from this time, and were formed by braided river systems eroding the mountainous region now lying to the south (see Bibliography - Ref No 4). The basis of the Armorican region we know today was now, geologically speaking, complete; but an ocean basin still separated our region from southern Britain. There is evidence of sedimentation in this sea in north-west France and south-west England, but the Palaeozoic history of the Channel Islands is largely unknown. The two regions finally became united during the Variscan Orogeny, around 300 million years ago. This caused further uplift and tilting of the Channel Islands, and gave rise to the formation of a series of lamprophyre dyke intrusions in Guernsey.

Minor Intrusions (Dykes and Veins)

The rocks of Guernsey are cut through by a large number of minor igneous intrusions known as dykes and veins. Some of these can be seen very strikingly from the air along the south coast (e.g. on the western side of Icart Point).

Dykes are sheet-like intrusions, usually a few metres wide and generally vertical or steeply dipping. They are typically of a dark grey medium-grained rock, known as dolerite, (of similar composition to gabbro and basalt), and formed as magma moved up toward the surface through cracks in the rock.

In Guernsey, there have been numerous phases of dyke intrusion, including dolerite, micro-diorite and lamprophyre, ranging in age from Pentevrian to Variscan. The earliest, Pentevrian dykes are now no more than darker bands within the Icart gneiss. During the Cadomian Orogeny, several phases of dyke intrusion (dolerites and micro-diorites) have been identified, especially in the south and west of the island, whilst the youngest of all the dyke intrusions - the Variscan lamprophyres - cut through all the older Pentevrian and younger Cadomian rocks alike.

Veins are smaller sheet-like intrusions, generally formed by crystallisation of mineral material from hot solutions, and typically associated with the later stages of cooling and crystallisation of granitic magmas. At the surface, such fluids may erupt as geysers (e.g. in Yellowstone Park, USA at the present day). In Guernsey, such veins comprise three main types: aplites, pegmatites and quartz veins. Aplites are fine-grained, pale pinkish veins which typically cut through granites and their surroundings (e.g. at L'Erée, itinerary 3). Pegmatites, on the other hand, are very coarse-grained indeed, often containing crystals of several centimetres in length. Quartz veins commonly occur along faults where fluids escaping from depth have deposited masses of this hard, white mineral. The most spectacular example is the large quartz vein extending from Pied du Mur (alternatively and erroneously called Marble Bay) to Petit Port in the south-east corner of the island, but numerous other examples occur. Some veins contain a variety of other minerals, such as the sickly green mineral epidote. At Moulin Huet and on Herm, quartz veins have been found to contain small quantities of copper and lead ores, whilst on Little Sark, similar veins were once mined for silver.

The Shaping of the Island

By around 250 million years ago, the Armorican and Cornubian (south-west England) regions had been welded into one by the events of the Variscan Orogeny, yet soon began to be torn apart again as the present-day North Atlantic opened, separating north-west Europe from North America. The result of this tension was to cause down-faulting and re-submergence of what is now the western Channel region during the ensuing Mesozoic Era. Thus, to the west and north of the Channel Islands, the sea is floored by thick sequences of Jurassic and Cretaceous sediments, in which oil (though not in large quantities) has been found.

It is likely that Guernsey remained above sea level throughout most, if not all, of the Mesozoic. The sea, however, was probably never far away, and characteristic chalk deposits of this age crop out on the sea floor only a few miles north of Guernsey. At the end of Cretaceous times, (about 65 million years ago), the sea receded once more so that Guernsey was probably again part of a single European landmass.

During the ensuing Tertiary Era, the sea encroached from time to time across the area, so that at some times during the last 65 million years the Channel Islands might have appeared as hills rising above a dry plain, whilst at others they appeared as islands not unlike the present day. Indeed, around 5-10 million years ago, sea level must have attained a height of some 90m (300ft) above its present level, causing the tops of the islands to be planed off as a large wave-cut platform now forming the flat plateau of Guernsey's "higher parishes" around the airport.

To the north and west, this plateau drops to a lower level at about 60m (200ft); this plateau forms much of the Parishes of St. Andrew's, St. Saviour's and St. Peter's. The plateau tops of Sark and Herm correspond to the two levels respectively.

The reasons for these great changes in sea-level are not yet fully understood, but it is generally agreed that they may be associated with variations in the rate of sea-floor spreading as the Atlantic Ocean opened up during the Tertiary Era.

The final events which shaped present-day Guernsey, and gave rise to its most recent rocks, began with the worldwide climatic cooling which heralded the start of the Quaternary Era some 2 million years ago. This change in global climate may have been the result of the shifting positions of the continents, reducing the circulation of ocean currents and thermally isolating the poles. As the polar regions cooled so the ice caps began to grow, and the Earth's climate became both cooler and more unstable. In Guernsey, the climate varied from arctic tundra to sub-tropical, as ice sheets repeatedly advanced from and retreated to the north (although they never actually reached as far south as the Channel Islands). Associated with the periodic advance and retreat of ice sheets, the sea-level around the islands also varied considerably. As ice accumulated during cold periods the sea-level fell, so that the islands stood out as hills above the barren tundra plain connecting them with France, whilst in warmer times sea-levels rose, often reaching levels higher than those of the present day. The threat of rising sea-level is by no means a new one!

During the periods of Arctic cold, little vegetation would have survived. Frost-shattered rock became embedded in the permafrost soils, but in warmer weather this material must have melted and slumped downslope (a process known as solifluction) to infill many small valleys with the mixture of shattered, angular rock fragments, sand and silt, which we now know as "head", and which can be seen in many bays forming steep, unstable cliffs such as those at Moulin Huet (Itinerary 1). During late spring and summer in these cold periods, meltwater must have carved out the deep, steep-sided valleys such as the Talbot Valley, St. Peter's Valley and Petit Bôt valley which today only contain small "misfit" streams incapable of such erosion. These valleys were carved down to a much lower sea-level than at the present day. As one flies into Guernsey from the west on a calm summer's day, these valleys (now filled with sand) can be seen to extend far out to sea beneath the clear water.

Not all the processes which took place during these "glacial" periods were erosional, however. At times, cold dry winds blowing across the north European glacial outwash plains brought with them dust and silt washed out from beneath the ice-sheets. These loess (locally "limon") deposits, formed mainly towards the end of the last (Devensian) ice advance, are the basis of the fertile soils in the southern half of Guernsey.

As has already been suggested, during the milder interglacial periods sea level was, at times, higher than today. These higher levels were accompanied by the erosion of wave-cut platforms and the deposition of beach material much as at the present day, forming a series of "Raised Beaches".

Three main raised beach platforms can be identified in Guernsey. The remains of the highest of these, at around 30m (100ft) above present sea-level, are fragmentary but can be seen in places around Rocquaine Bay and along the Cobo road between the bottom of the Rohais and Saumarez Park, where Rectory Hill marks the old cliff line. Remains of raised beach material at this level are known from Les Vardes and St. Germain quarries. At Les Tielles, on the south coast, a small cave in the cliff may also date from this time, around 200,000 years ago in the Hoxnian Interglacial period.

The 18m (60ft) raised beach platform is spectacularly clear in Rocquaine Bay (Itinerary 4) where it stretches from Pezeries Point at Pleinmont to Fort Grey and beyond, extending inland about a quarter of a mile. It is backed by a fine "fossil" cliff line rising up to the "200ft" plateau level. The age of this raised beach level is thought to be about 120,000 years or so. Other fragments of this raised beach appear at many places around the coast and also further inland in the lower parts of the island. The 8m (25ft) raised beach is superbly exposed on L'Erée headland near the slipway to Lihou island (Itinerary 3); it possibly dates from around 80-100,000 years ago, from the Ipswichian Interglacial. As on the present day beaches, the 8m raised beach contains numerous flint pebbles as well as local rock types. The origin of these flints is uncertain, as there is no evidence that the Chalk Sea of Upper Cretaceous times (flints are only formed in chalk) ever covered Guernsey. The most plausible explanation is that flints eroded from chalk deposits to the north and west of Guernsey in times of low sea-level during glacial periods were slowly washed up by wave action as sea-levels rose during the warmer interglacial interludes. An alternative suggestion is that the flints were deposited from melting ice floes.

Whatever the explanation, early Man made use of these flints, and several finds of flint tools have been made, suggesting Man's intermittent occupation of the Channel Islands over at least the last 100,000 years or so.

During the last 10,000 years, since the retreat of the (Devensian) ice sheets, sea-level has slowly risen, and the islands gradually became cut off once more from France. Guernsey, along with Herm and Sark, were undoubtedly the first to become isolated, as suggested by the lack of certain animals such as moles (common in Alderney and Jersey). Evidence of lower sea-level in the relatively recent past is sometimes exposed on our west coast for example at Vazon, where peat deposits, normally buried beneath beach sand, are occasionally uncovered by storms. These beds contain remains of many familiar trees such as birch, oak and alder, and have been dated as being about 5,000 years old. In 1990, a storm revealed a tree trunk at Vazon with marks suggesting that it could have been felled by means of flint tools. To the north of Guernsey and Herm, ancient burial sites (passage graves) have been reported by divers, once built on land but now long since submerged. Even during historic times, a pebble ridge once linking Herm and Jethou has been washed away, and man's present efforts at sea defences can be at best regarded as temporary.

The youngest geological feature of the islands are the deposits of windblown sand in the north of Guernsey and Herm, not perhaps of great geological interest, but providing some of the best golfing and sunbathing to be had in the islands.

ITINERARIES OF GEOLOGICAL INTEREST

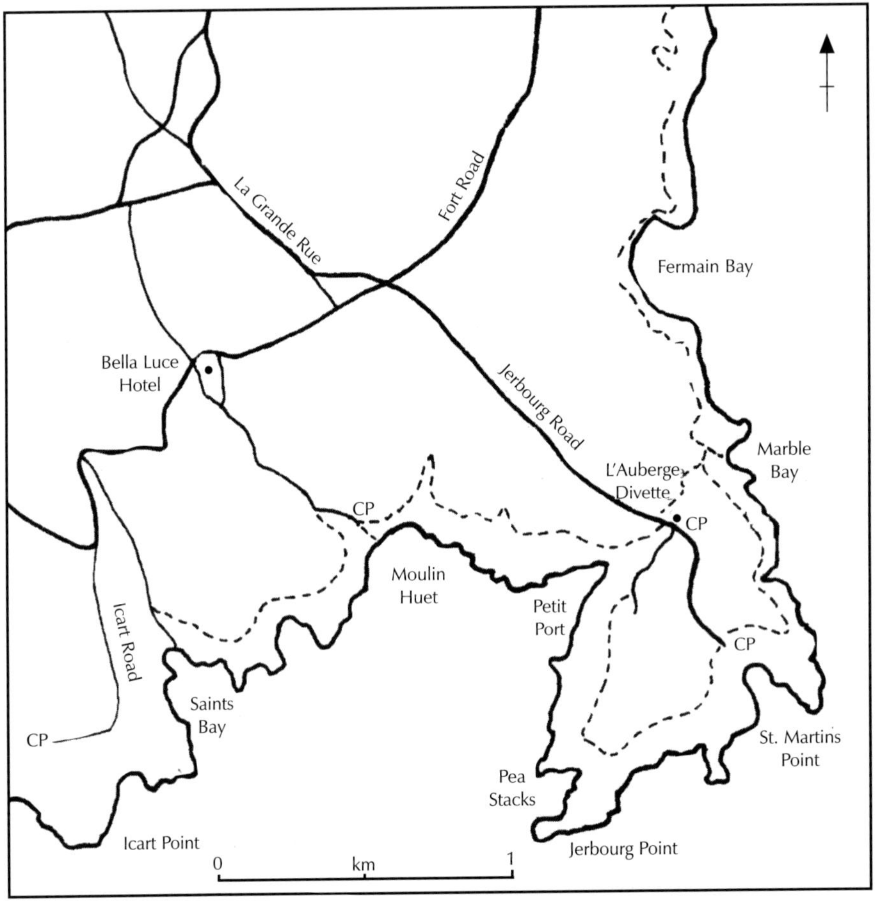

Itineraries 1 & 2

Moulin Huet - Marble Bay

Eastern Coast of Moulin Huet Bay

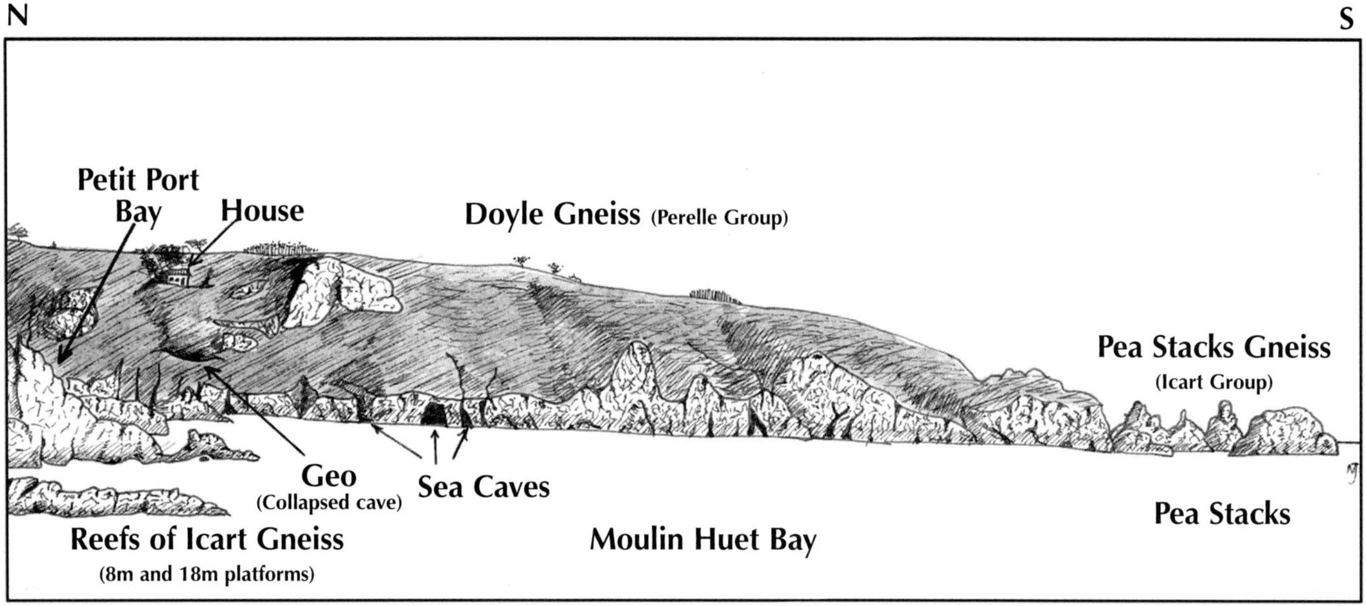

Fig. 1

ITINERARY 1 - MOULIN HUET

Moulin Huet (pronounced moolin-wet) Bay is located in the south-eastern part of the island. It is easily accessible, has a car park and cafe located close by, and is best visited below half tide.

The bay lies at the foot of a pleasant wooded valley which descends from the Bella Luce Hotel. The valley has been eroded along a fault, a zone of weakened rock probably eroded by meltwater streams during the "Ice Age", but now containing only a small "misfit" stream.

Descend the path from the car park to the small platform with railings just above the beach. From this point an excellent view is obtained to the south-east, of the Pea Stacks and the cliffs on the east side of Petit Port bay, shown in Fig. 1. There are several sea caves in this cliff, mostly eroded along small faults or other weaknesses, including one cave (below the house on the cliff) whose roof has collapsed to form a blowhole or "geo". The same process of wave erosion along geological weaknesses has led to the formation of the Pea Stacks. Also visible immediately below this vantage point is a "fossil" wave-cut platform, corresponding with the 8m raised beach level and now being gradually dissected by a series of inlets as the sea slowly cuts a new wave-cut platform down to present-day low tide level. Examination of these inlets invariably shows that they are being eroded along zones of weaker rock such as dykes or faults.

Descend the narrow slipway to the right and cross the beach to the base of the cliff on the far side of the bay. Here at the foot of the valley is an excellent exposure of head, composed of angular frost-shattered fragments embedded in a matrix of yellow-brown sand and silt (loess). Indistinct layering is visible, reflecting successive periods of solifluction as the deposit accumulated. (See Fig 2.)

Near the foot of the slipway, the Icart Gneiss can be examined. In this area, the large pink feldspars have a squashed appearance and the light and dark bands of minerals give this rock its special character. A careful search of the gneiss reveals occasional dark streaks, possibly remains of dykes intruded into the original granite before it was changed to gneiss through metamorphism. Close by the slipway the gneiss is cut by two younger dykes (one dolerite and one lamprophyre) which, being softer rock than the gneiss, are being eroded by the sea leaving gullies. The grey dolerite dyke shows a "chilled margin" - a finer grained edge (often rather flaky-looking) reflecting more rapid crystallisation of the magma where it was in contact with the cool surrounding rock.

Head Deposit, West side of Moulin Huet

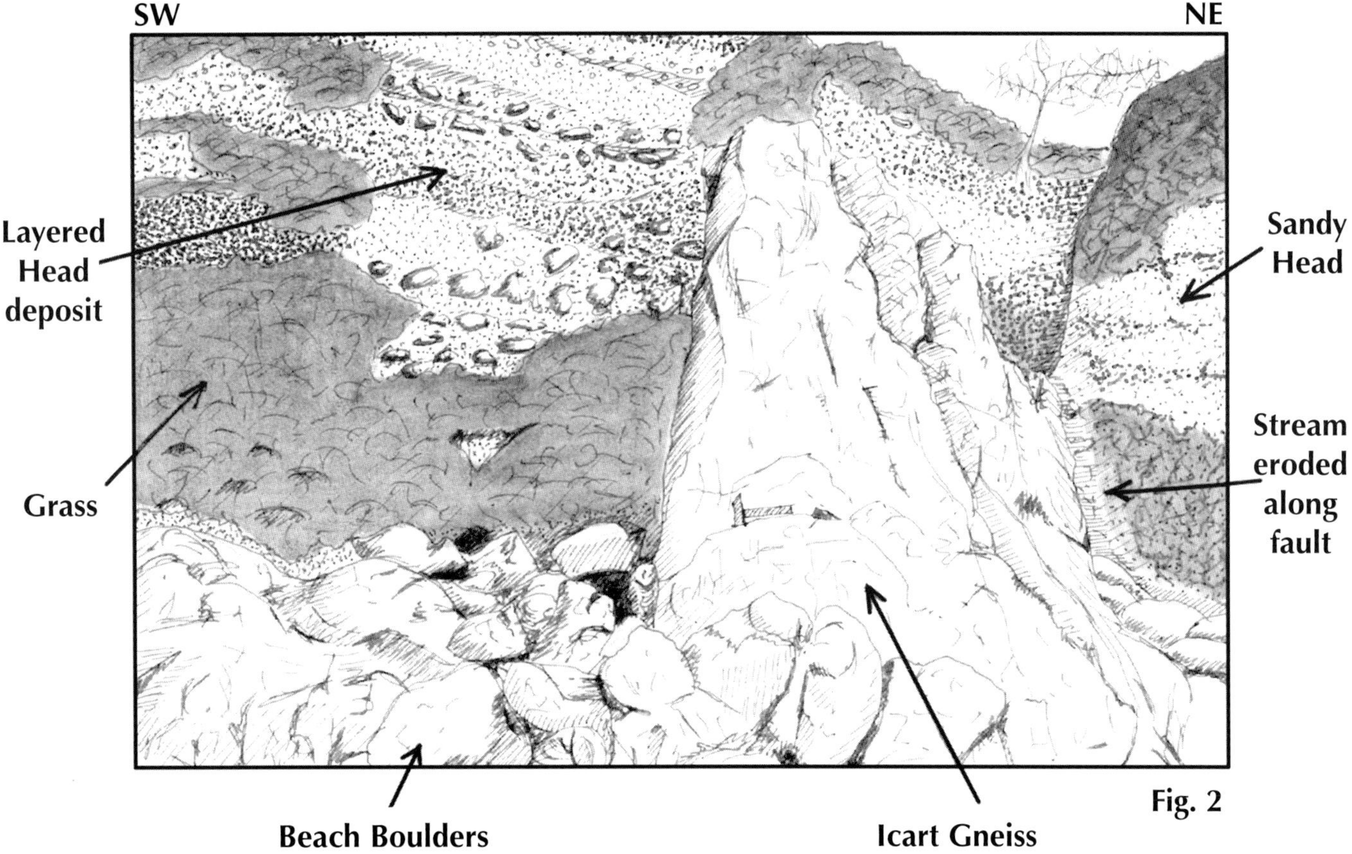

Fig. 2

Return to the platform and descend the steps on its eastern side. At the foot of the main flight of steps, more head deposits can be seen at the cliff base. Of interest here are the deposits of ironstone precipitated by ground water percolating through the head, slowly cementing the fragments together to form a hard rock mass.

Fig 3 illustrates the cliff base at the foot of the remaining rock steps down to the beach. This gully shows numerous geological features. Its western side is made up of a Variscan lamprophyre dyke, which is very distinctive, being a muddy brown colour and displaying a "honeycombed" appearance; it dips at about 50° to the north-east. Beyond the dyke at the foot of the cliff is a ledge, which is a remnant of the 8m wave-cut platform, with a clear "fossil" wave-cut notch above it. At the top of the gully is a pebbly raised beach deposit overlain by more head deposits, the two being distinguishable by the shape of the pebbles which they contain.

A few metres further east, a sea cave, eroded along two small faults, contains remnants of possibly two raised beach deposits. The 8m beach is to be found at the back of the cave at about head height. Towards the roof of the cave, another deposit can be seen (see Fig 4). It is questionable as to whether this is part of the 18m raised beach, or a higher part of the 8m beach, but the origin of both deposits is clear

Continuing eastward, there are present-day wave-cut notches visible at the base of the cliff in several places. There are also two inlets eroded along steeply-dipping dolerite dykes. The second inlet shows two dykes and a small fault, as shown in Fig 5. The fault may have provided the plane of weakness for the dolerite intrusion which then split in two directions upwards. The main dyke is not quite visible, being hidden below the present beach level.

As you approach the small waterfall at the eastern side of the bay, you may notice small white veins of quartz in the beach boulders and cliff base. There are also veins of yellow-green epidote. These boulders have been eroded from the faulted, weakened and rather dangerous cliffs nearby. The mineral veins have formed as a result of hot fluids long ago escaping from depth along the zone of shattered rock, depositing chemicals from solution as their temperature and pressure decreased.The mineralised veins at Moulin Huet were at one time explored for copper minerals. Although a small mine was begun near here, it never proved economically viable, and was closed, it is said, when a local landowner threatened legal action as a result of his well drying up!

At low spring tide, it is possible to continue along the coast to Petit Port, itself of considerable geological interest. This bay is also mentioned in Itinerary 2. If the bay is visited from Moulin Huet great care should be taken not to be cut off by the rising tide.

Gully at foot of steps, Moulin Huet

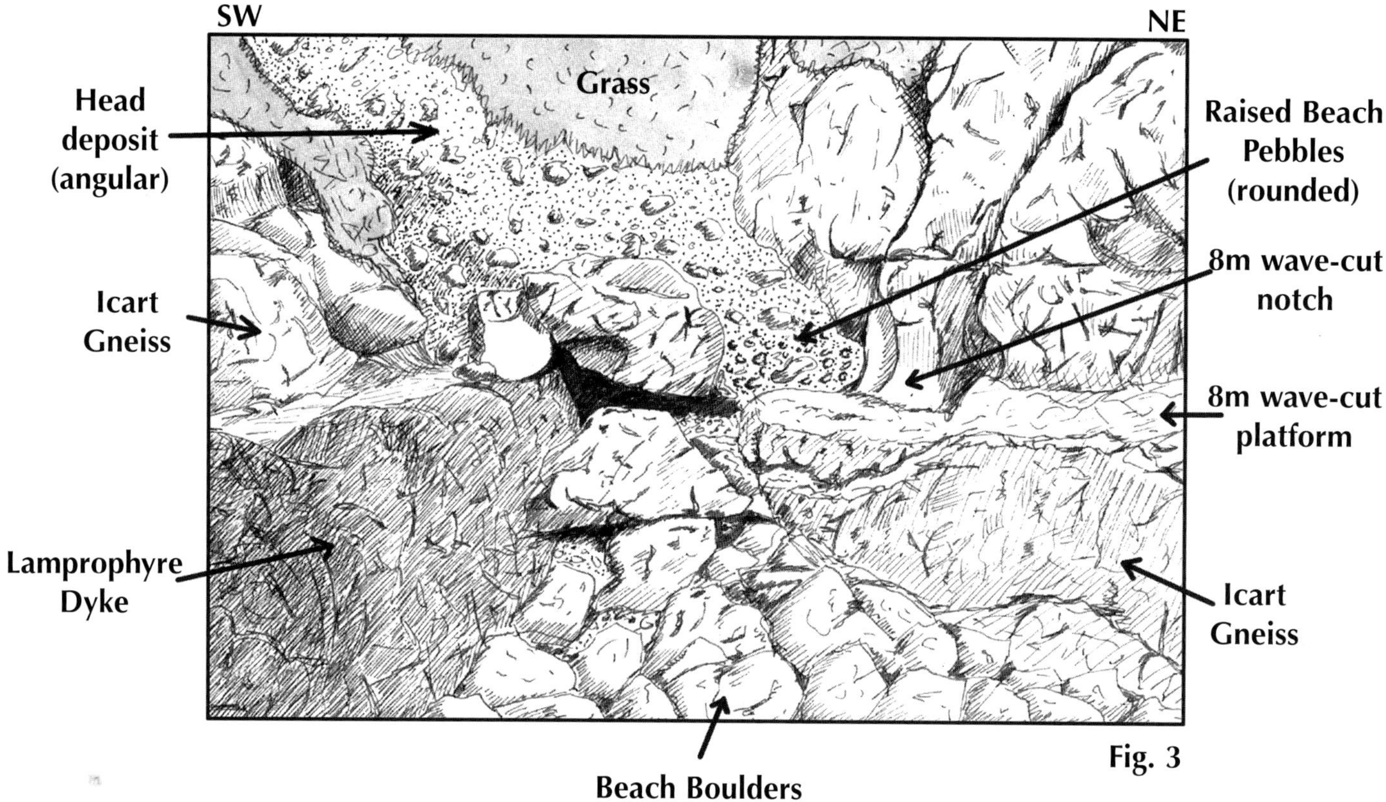

Fig. 3

Small Cave at Moulin Huet

Fig. 4

Fault and Dykes:
Inlet 50m W of Le Vallon Waterfall,
Moulin Huet.

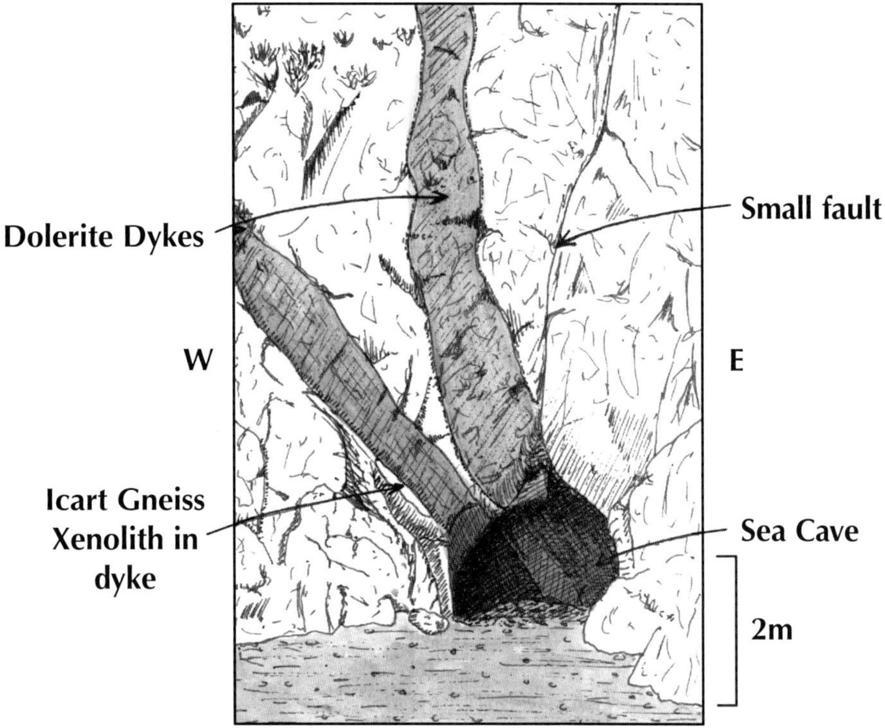

Fig. 5

ITINERARY 2 - MARBLE BAY AND PETIT PORT

The Jerbourg peninsula forms the south-eastern corner of Guernsey. It is a popular area with locals and visitors alike, the cliff walks affording fine views of the other Channel Islands. The wooded slopes on its eastern side are carpeted with spring bluebells whilst on the western side the inaccessible Pea Stacks are a nesting ground for many sea birds and hence of interest to ornithologists. The same area is also of considerable geological interest.

Begin this excursion from L'Auberge Divette car park. Take the footpath immediately to the north of the pub and descend to Bec du Nez which is a small promontory just to to the north of Marble Bay. Descend the steps from the paved battery to the slipway and traverse around the headland to the right. Some scrambling over rocks is required at this point so care should be taken. The headland at this level is composed of fractured Icart Gneiss with the large pink feldspar crystals having been severely squashed. This is due to the presence of a fault zone which runs from Marble Bay through the Jerbourg peninsula to Petit Port. A number of dolerite dykes can be found cutting the gneiss in this area with an approximate trend NE-SW. Tracing these dykes can be difficult since they are frequently cut by shear zones where the rock has been crushed by movement and hence the dykes have become dislocated.

The southern side of Bec du Nez forms a rock shelf, part of the 18m wave-cut platform (see Fig. 6). Walk along this platform towards Marble Bay. In the base of the cliff above this platform is evidence of the 18m raised beach, overlain and partially obscured by Head deposits. Of particular interest, at the base of this upper cliff, is a dolerite dyke which has enclosed slices or 'xenoliths" of Icart Gneiss. These slices were broken off the country rock as the molten dolerite was intruded.

Turn back towards the slipway and follow the cliff path around to Marble Bay. The descent from the rock platform directly to the beach is recommended only for mountaineers!

Marble Bay was formed as a result of the sea eroding along the zone of weak, fractured rock associated with the fault mentioned above. In places within the bay, the rock is heavily veined by white quartz, whilst on the southern side the bay is flanked by a massive single quartz vein some 2-3m thick, which dips steeply to the north. It is the presence of all this white vein quartz which has given the bay its quite erroneous name. Close examination of the smaller veins

Bec du Nez. (Marble Bay)

Fig. 6

within the bay shows that they have been sheared and deformed by further movement along the fault, giving rise to a complex mass of broken rock and dislocated veins

The north side of the bay has a couple of fine sea caves, eroded along minor faults; the main cave ends in a collapsed blowhole, or "geo", shown in Fig 6. Another marked feature here is the fine wave cut notch seen at the base of the cliff.

On the south side of the bay is a rock platform (a continuation of the rock shelf on the northern side), which can be climbed below half tide. The edge of this platform is composed of the massive quartz vein mentioned previously. Care should be taken here as algae-covered quartz is very slippery when wet. The vein also marks the fault boundary between the Icart Gneiss and the Doyle Gneiss. The latter is very similar to the Icart gneiss but lacks the large characteristic pink feldspar crystals.

Some steps lead up from the rock shelf nearby. Near the bottom of these steps are a few large boulders, composed mainly of the rather finer-grained rock type know as schist. Close examination of the layering reveals cross-cutting features (Fig 7) which, although not conclusive, suggest the origin of this rock as a sediment laid down by running water (perhaps a river, or offshore tidal currents). These schists form part of the Jerbourg Metasediment group, and are undoubtedly the oldest rocks in Guernsey, formed more than 2,500 million years ago.

The rock platform on the south side of Marble Bay may be followed further south to a sandy inlet at Divette. Here, on the south side of the inlet is a good exposure of the metasediment. The banded schists at this location show much small-scale folding, illustrating how the original rock has been distorted by later earth movements. Near the base of the steps leading to the inlet is a zone where slices of pink granite have been injected into the metasediments.

From this point it is possible to follow a path to St. Martin's Point, and then continue around Jerbourg Point (with fine views of the Pea Stacks) to Petit Port. Alternatively, you may return directly to L'Auberge Divette. It is well worth taking the short walk westward along the path from the car park to the west of the Doyle Monument, and turning to the right so as to gain a view from the cliff top overlooking Petit Port from the south (see cover photograph). Here, once again, the large quartz vein seen in Marble Bay is exposed in the cliff top - it is clearly this hard, resistant feature that forms the ridge upon which the Doyle Monument was built and which once formed the defensive bulwark of a Neolithic Fort of which traces still remain. The cover photograph also shows, on the left, the remains of what must have once been a sea-stack at a time of higher sea level about a hundred thousand years ago.

Jerbourg Metasediment, Divette (Marble Bay).

Fig. 7

The descent to Petit Port involves a large number of steps, and is only advised for the hale and hearty. It is, however, worth the effort as this is one of Guernsey's finest and most sheltered beaches as well as an area of geological interest. At the time of writing the path was temporarily closed due to a rock fall, but has more recently been re-opened. It is unfortunate that this path is sited on a zone of weakened rock next to a fault.

Near the foot of the path (Fig 8), a narrow cleft in the rock has been eroded along the fault mentioned at Marble Bay. The intrepid geologist who enters this narrow cave can observe rough score marks (known as slickensides) caused by movement along the fault.

There are several other interesting sea-caves in the cliffs on either side of the bay, shown in Fig 1 and Fig 8. One large cave on the eastern side appears to have been eroded along two levels at different times in the past, and culminates in a spectacular collapsed "blowhole" (geo) shown in Fig 1. On the western side of the bay there are some spectacular dykes exposed in the cliff (Fig.8). Petit Port is a good place to explore whilst the family build sand-castles!

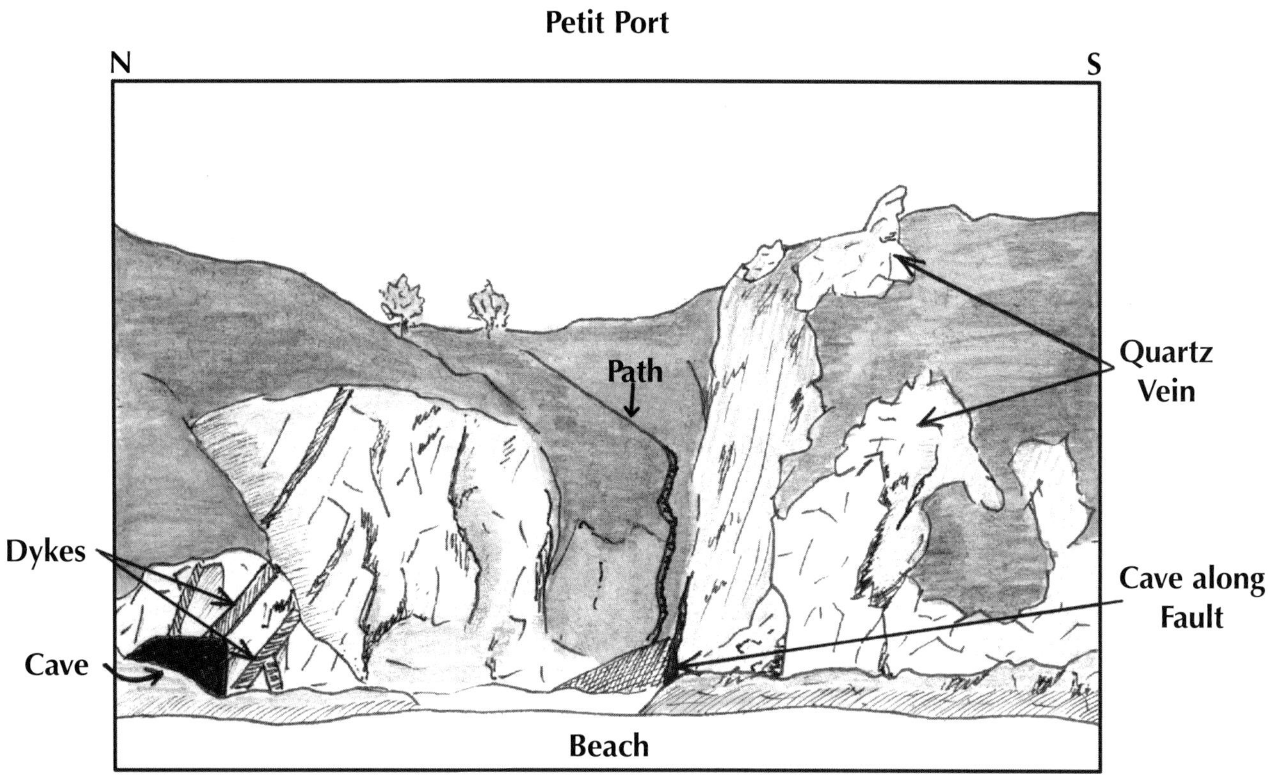
Petit Port
N
S
Path
Quartz
Vein
Dykes
Cave
Cave along
Fault
Beach

Fig. 8

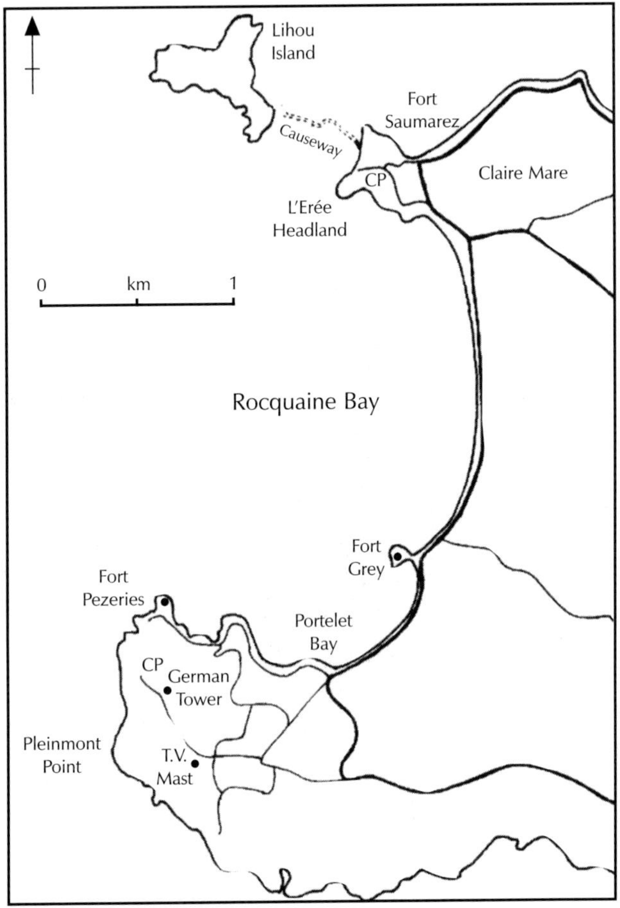

Itineraries 3 & 4

Pleinmont - L'Erée

Dolerite Dyke and Columnar Jointing
50m N of L'Erée Headland

Fig. 9

ITINERARY 3 - L'ERÉE HEADLAND

The low hill of the L'Erée headland, with its German observation tower built atop a Napoleonic coastal fort, stands out above the surrounding "marais" that form much of the west coast lowlands.

This route starts at the car park on L'Erée headland overlooking Lihou island. From there, walk down the slipway facing Lihou and turn to the left where a shallow cliff with a number of small coves extends around the headland. The cliffs in these coves are largely made up of the 8m raised beach material. Typically the lower part of the cliff is composed of rounded beach pebbles, sometimes displaying parallel alignment of their long axes as if they had been pushed up into a ridge by wave action. These pebbles are fairly well cemented together although it is possible to extract some pebbles since the cement is geologically recent. This deposit was laid down during the Ipswichian interglacial period approximately 120,000 years ago. Above this beach material is a much finer grained deposit resembling a light brown soil known as loess. This was probably laid down towards the end of the Devensian glacial period about 10,000 years ago.

Walk back towards the slipway, cross it and continue northwards along the beach towards a low grassy headland that is rapidly being eroded by the sea. En route to this headland are numerous outcrops of the L'Erée Granite, which is a distinctive igneous rock containing large pink megacrysts of feldspar. These crystals probably grew slowly after the main crystallisation of the granite due to the action of hot gases which "fed" the crystals enabling them to grow to 3 or 4cm long. Concentric rings of dark inclusions within such crystals mark stages in their slow growth. Radiometric dates of 646± 25 million years have been obtained from the L'Erée Granite confirming an early Cadomian age.

Having reached the headland, if tidal conditions permit, it is worth walking out across the beach in a north-westerly direction for approximately 50m to a rocky outcrop that stands out above the general level of the foreshore. Running through this outcrop of granite in a roughly east-west direction is a dark grey-brown dolerite dyke, approximately 3m wide. (Fig. 9) The dyke has a rather distinctive appearance due to the jointing pattern which is similar to that of Giant's Causeway in Northern Ireland, where the vertical joints produce numerous hexagonal columns. Here, however, the jointing pattern is almost horizontal, producing a staircase effect. Another feature of this dyke is the presence of a brittle, fine-grained "chilled margin" next to the granite, showing that the dolerite was intruded long after the granite had cooled down.

Recent Deposits at L'Erée

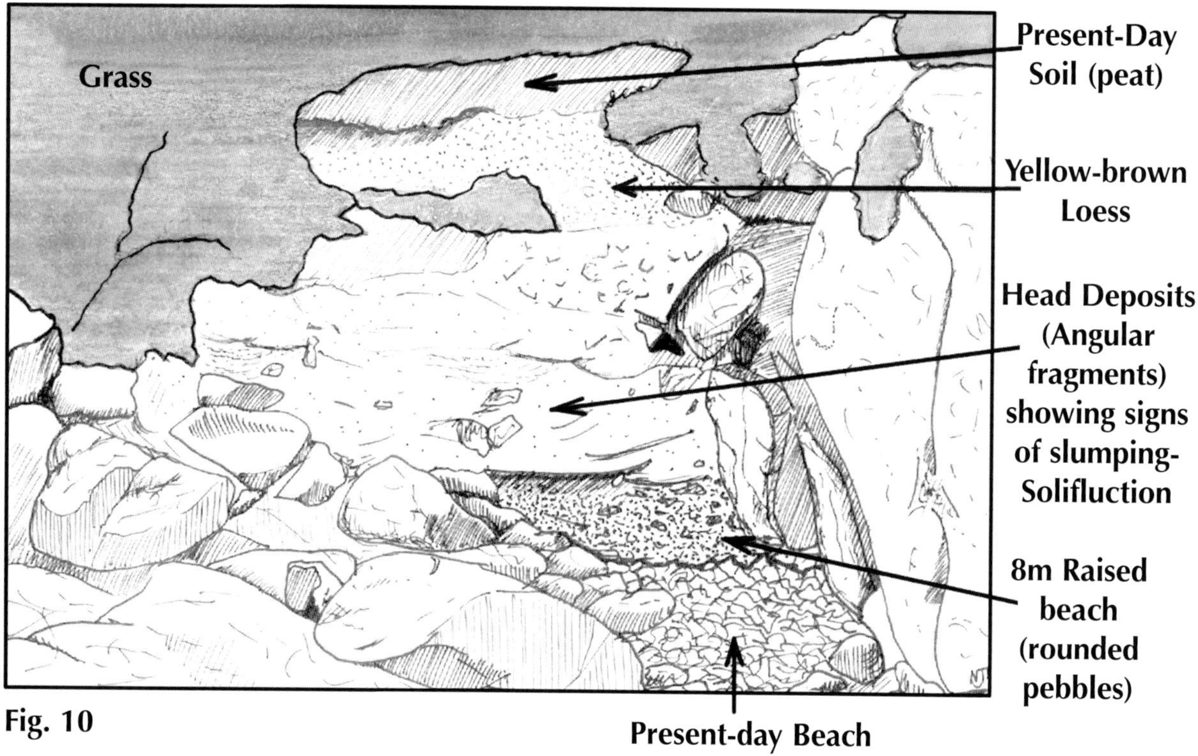

Fig. 10

Return to the headland which shows a fine exposure of the 8m Raised Beach, and continue along its northern shore below Fort Saumarez. Along this stretch of coast are several geological features of interest which are best seen following a line along the high water mark.

Around 50m east of the headland, a cleft in the cliff reveals a series of three layers - of raised beach, head and loess material (Fig 10) which illustrates clearly the age relationship between these - the oldest (Ipswichian Raised Beach) deposit being overlain by the progressively younger (Devensian) head and loess deposits. At several places nearby pink aplite veins can be seen cutting through the L'Erée Granite. Usually they are 10cm to 1m in thickness and represent a late stage of cooling when the magma had virtually crystallised and residual fluids escaped along cracks in the rock, depositing their dissolved mineral load as they cooled down. (Fig. 11)

In this same area there are also several dark patches within the granite varying in size from just a few centimetres to over a metre in length. These are known as xenoliths and they represent fragments of the original host rock. (Fig.12) They appear to be composed of rock similar to the Perelle Gneiss but have changed their character due to the heat of the granite magma. Some have almost disappeared and remain as "ghosts" having been virtually assimilated into the granite.

Continue onwards to the slipway below Fort Saumarez. To the east of this slipway, a large shingle bank extends towards Perelle, providing protection to the north of the Claire Mare - the lowland area which was the site of Guernsey's first aerodrome. This feature is a natural one built by the action of storm waves, albeit modified in recent years by the occasional JCB after storms have thrown pebbles onto the road which runs along the landward side of the bank.

At the eastern end of the bank below the sea wall an exposure of ancient peat can usually be seen. This peat contains much visible vegetable matter - leaves and stems - and pollen analysis has shown that it is composed largely of the remains of woodland (mainly birch, alder and oak) which grew on this site about 5,000 years ago, when sea level was several metres below that of the present day. Below the peat is a layer of light grey clay in which the plants of the peat layer were rooted. These peat deposits are also discussed on Page13.

From here return to the car park via the road that goes over the headland.

Aplite veins in L'Erée Granite

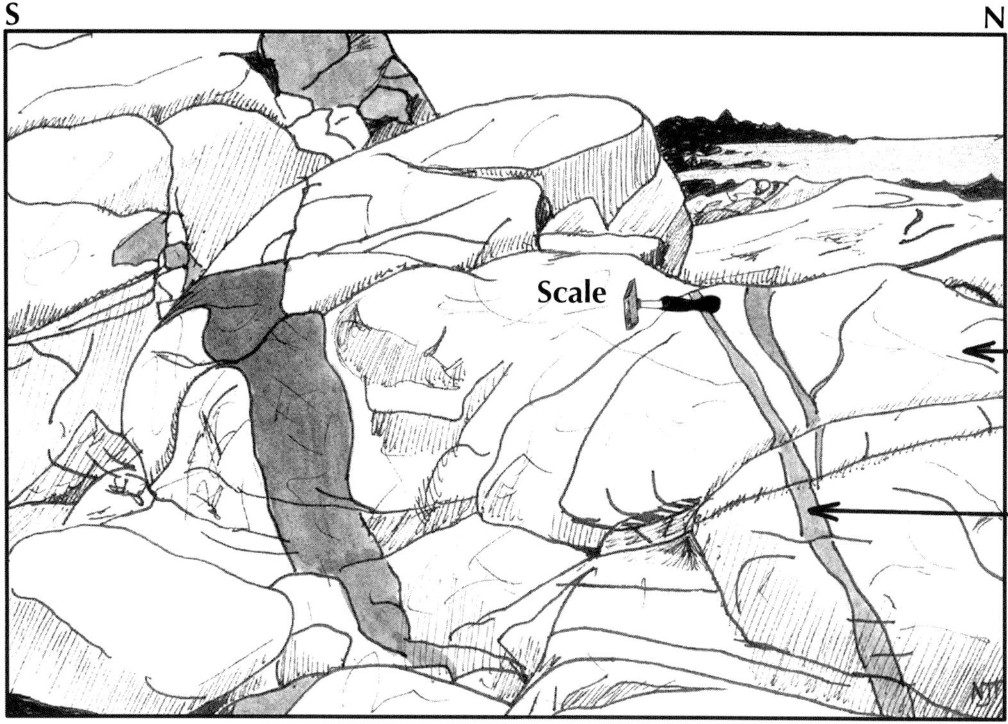

Fig. 11

Xenolith of Perelle Gneiss in L'Erée Granite

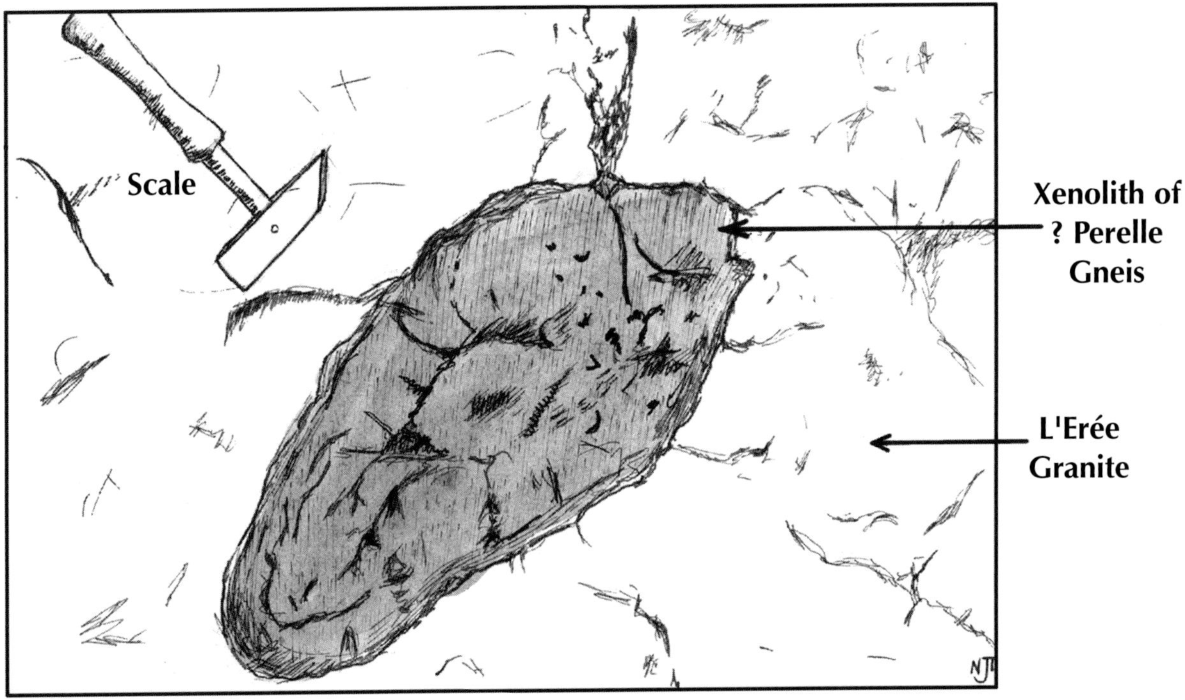

Fig. 12

Pleinmont Headland

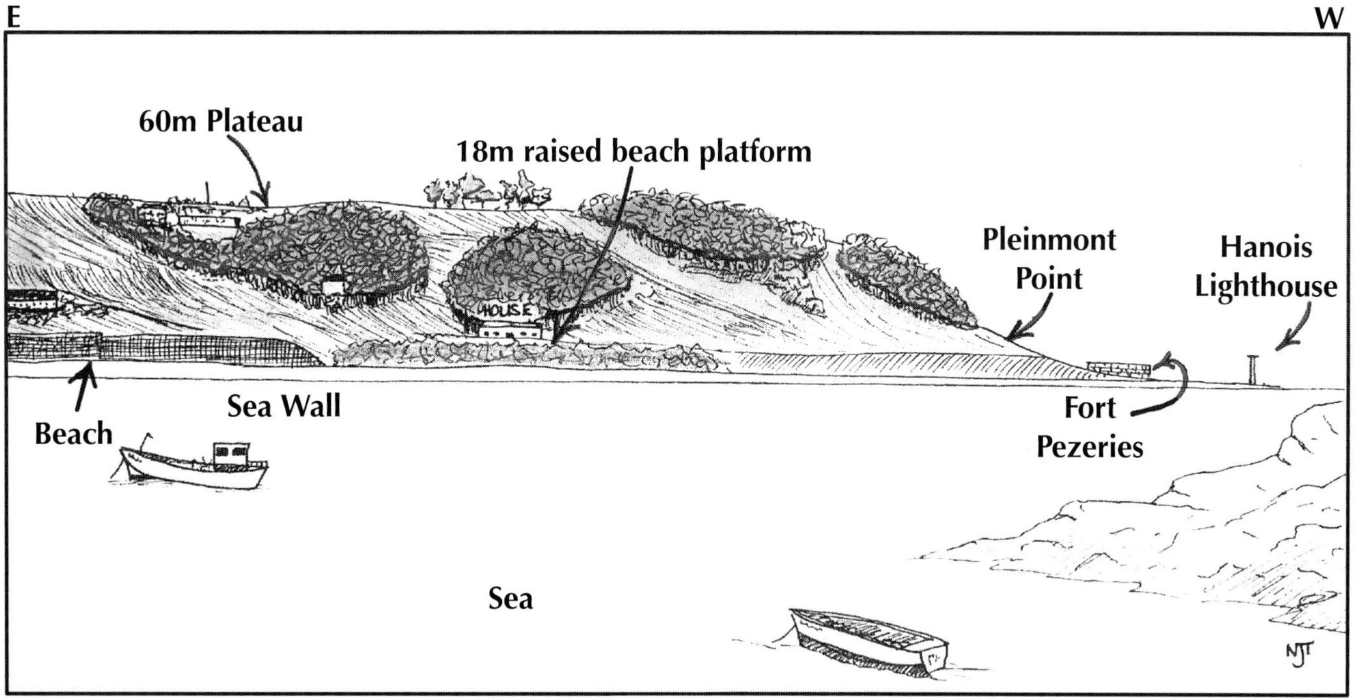

Fig. 13

ITINERARY 4 - ROCQUAINE BAY AND PLEINMONT

Rocquaine Bay is arguably one of Guernsey's most attractive, with both sandy beaches and rocky reefs, and in summer it is all the more picturesque for the plethora of small fishing boats anchored in its shelter. The treacherous offshore reefs (eroded remains of older wave-cut platforms) have caused many shipwrecks in the past, as a visit to the Fort Grey Maritime Museum in the centre of the bay will attest.

The beach is backed by a low-lying coastal "marais" - once salt marsh protected by sand dunes; the dunes have been removed for building materials necessitating, in turn, the building of artificial sea defences later strengthened by the German occupiers in World War II. The marais are, in turn, backed by the ancient (pre-glacial) cliff line which now forms wooded slopes at the foot of which nestle the oldest settlements - above the marshes, but sheltered from storms and served by fresh-water springs.

Pleinmont Point, with its varied flora, ancient remains and fortifications dating from the sixteenth century to World War II is also a location of scenic and geological interest. A geological excursion can begin at Fort Pezeries (see Fig 13) which may be reached on foot from Portelet (the southern end of Rocquaine Bay) or by driving onto the top of the headland, past the television transmitter to the car park by the German observation tower on the point. A path from here descends towards Fort Pezeries and Portelet.

The beach on the west side of Fort Pezeries exposes the contact between a rather compressed and sheared version (almost a gneiss) of the L'Eree Granite and the dull brownish-grey Pleinmont Metasediment. A walk along the foreshore shows this contact to be a complex one, with slivers of metasediment and granite interfingering, and much evidence of lateral movement which probably accompanied or followed soon after the intrusion of the granite.

The Pleinmont Metasediment is thought to be around 700-1000 million years old. Little can be said about its origin, save that it was probably a silty marine sediment. It is virtually featureless and has been strongly deformed, as shown by a small s-fold in a pale band (possibly an aplite vein) on the top of Compass Rock about 100m west of Fort Pezeries.

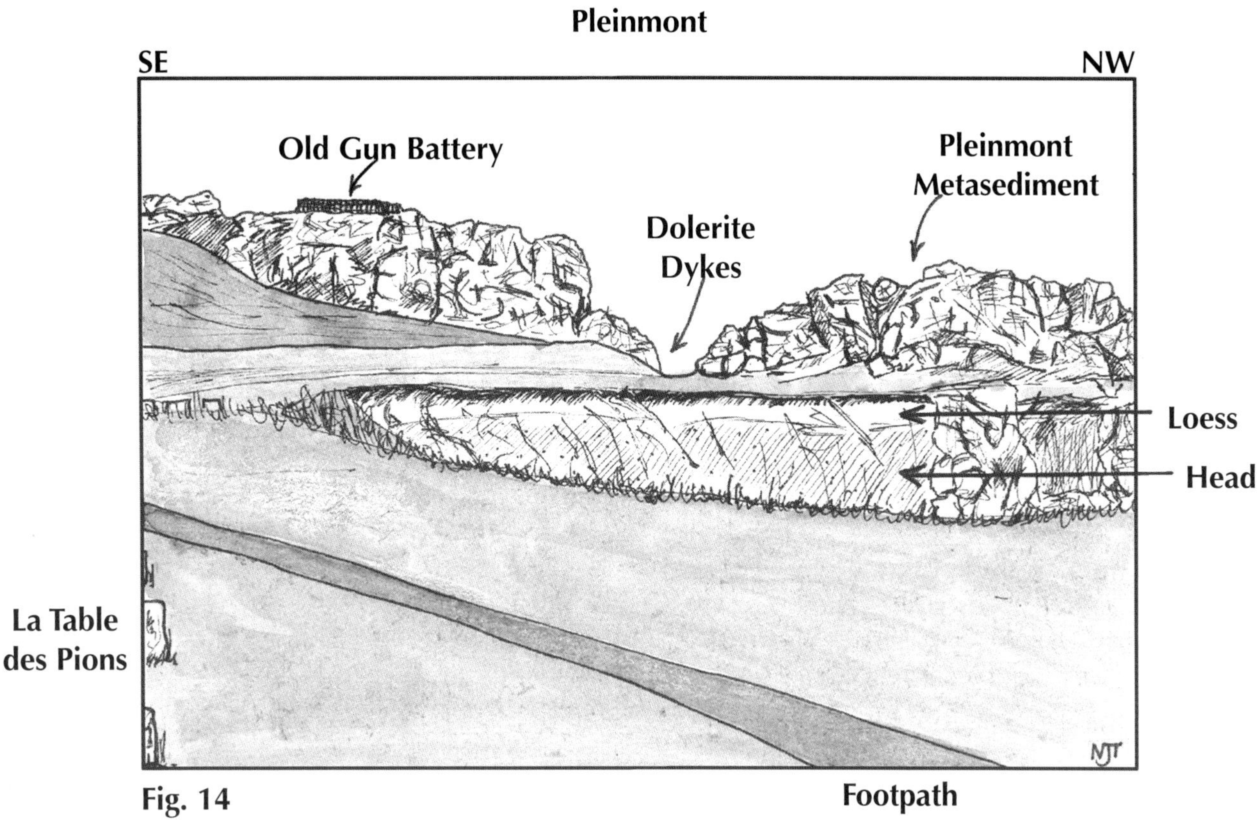
Pleinmont
SE
NW
Old Gun Battery
Pleinmont
Metasediment
Dolerite
Dykes
Loess
Head
La Table
des Pions
NJT
Footpath

Fig. 14

The low cliffs of the bay just described are composed of head material which has slumped down onto the 8m wave-cut platform, as are the cliffs above the slipway in the next bay. Returning to the top via the slipway, you will find yourself close to the Table des Pions (an ancient stone circle). The view shown in Fig 14 is seen from this point. The bluff of rock shown in the drawing is probably a relic of a higher "raised beach" level; the gap in that bluff is part natural and part man-made, following a pair of thin dolerite dykes which cut through the metasediment. They have weathered more rapidly, with help from soldiers a couple of centuries ago to give access to a coastal battery in the next bay. The dykes can easily be picked out where the path cuts through the gap.

The bay to the west of the bluff forms a pleasing natural amphitheatre; it is again part-filled by head deposits. Below the gun battery on the far side, a pebble-filled gully running out to sea marks another dolerite dyke eroded by the sea. From here the coast is inaccessible but a direct path leads back up the slope to the German Tower.

On the south coast, about 1½ miles east of Pleinmont, the intrepid explorer might wish to visit the cave known as the Creux Mahie. It must be emphasised, however, that this cave is difficult of access as the path leading to it is now in a rather dangerous condition - and also hard to find. Ironically, there was a time earlier in the 20th century, when guided tours of the cave were offered to tourists! It lies at the head of a deep gully about ½ mile east of Les Tielles, and is eroded along one of several faults and dykes in the south coast cliffs. The cave floor, however, is above the reach of present-day high tides (even allowing for the rock fall which partly blocks its entrance) and its several hundred feet in length suggests that it was carved over a long period of high sea level, probably during the last interglacial and, perhaps, even earlier.

Although no archaeological work has yet been undertaken at Creux Mahie, there may one day be some interesting finds. A similar site in Jersey, La Cotte de St. Brelade, has yielded a wealth of Palaeolithic remains including tools and many bones of bison, cave bear, mammoth and other animals. It is interesting to speculate on the possibilities of excavating Creux Mahie, but serious consideration reveals a very daunting, and dangerous, task.

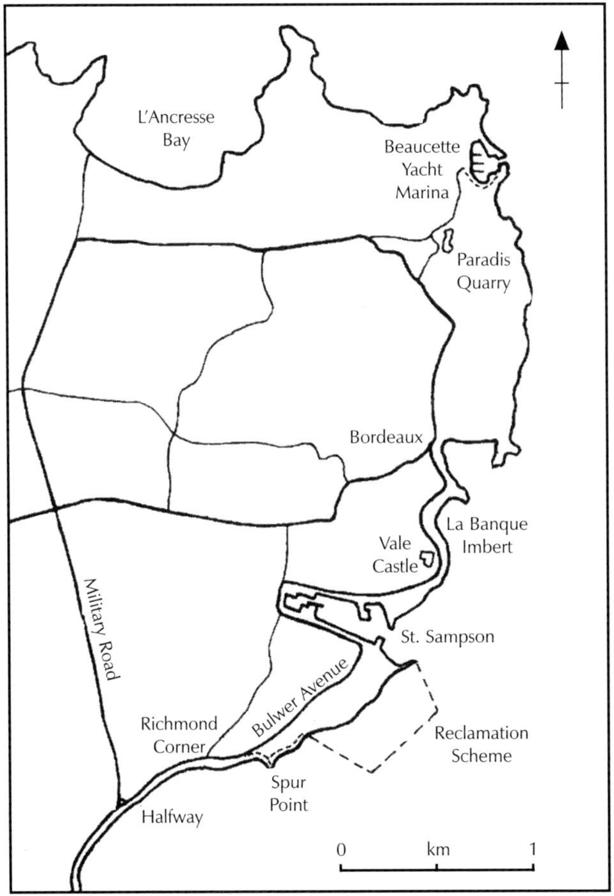

Itinerary 5
St. Sampson - Beaucette

ITINERARY 5 - SPUR BAY AND BEAUCETTE

Guernsey's east coast includes a wide variety of scenery. To the south of St. Peter Port, the cliff walks through pleasant woodland towards St. Martin's Point are among the most popular in the island (see Itinerary 2). To the north, the lowland scenery of Belle Greve Bay is not so attractive, the rocks of the foreshore being composed of the rather sombre St. Peter Port Gabbro. The industrial scenery of St. Sampson's then gives way to a more attractive coastline around the Vale Castle, Bordeaux harbour, and northward to Beaucette Marina.

The rocks of northern Guernsey, including the St. Peter Port Gabbro and the Bordeaux Diorite were extensively quarried during the nineteenth century. The export of this stone provided the mainstay of Guernsey's economy for many years.

The Vale parish, in particular, has a great number of abandoned quarries - many of which are now used for water storage. Others have been used as rubbish dumps as at Bordeaux, and one has been converted into the marina at Beaucette.

From a geological point of view the whole coastline north of St. Peter Port is of interest. This Itinerary suggests three places of special importance - Spur Bay, La Banque Imbert and Beaucette Marina.

From the road side car park at the southern end of Bulwer Avenue take the path out to the small grassy headland, past the German bunker that overlooks Belle Greve Bay. At the headland turn left and cross the small bay known as Spur Bay. Near the high water mark in the centre of the bay are several small outcrops of grey rock. A close inspection of this rock shows considerable differences from the rocks encountered in previous itineraries. Although the rock, known as gabbro, is coarsely crystalline indicating an igneous origin, many of the crystals are aligned into bands. The dark bands are composed predominantly of black hornblende and the lighter bands of grey feldspar. The layered appearance of this rock is a distinctive feature which is frequently seen in other gabbros around the world. The dark bands are usually composed of large rounded crystals of hornblende surrounded by finer grey feldspar crystals. This variety is known as "Bird's Eye" gabbro (see Fig 15).

Layering of St. Peter Port, Gabbro, Spur Bay.

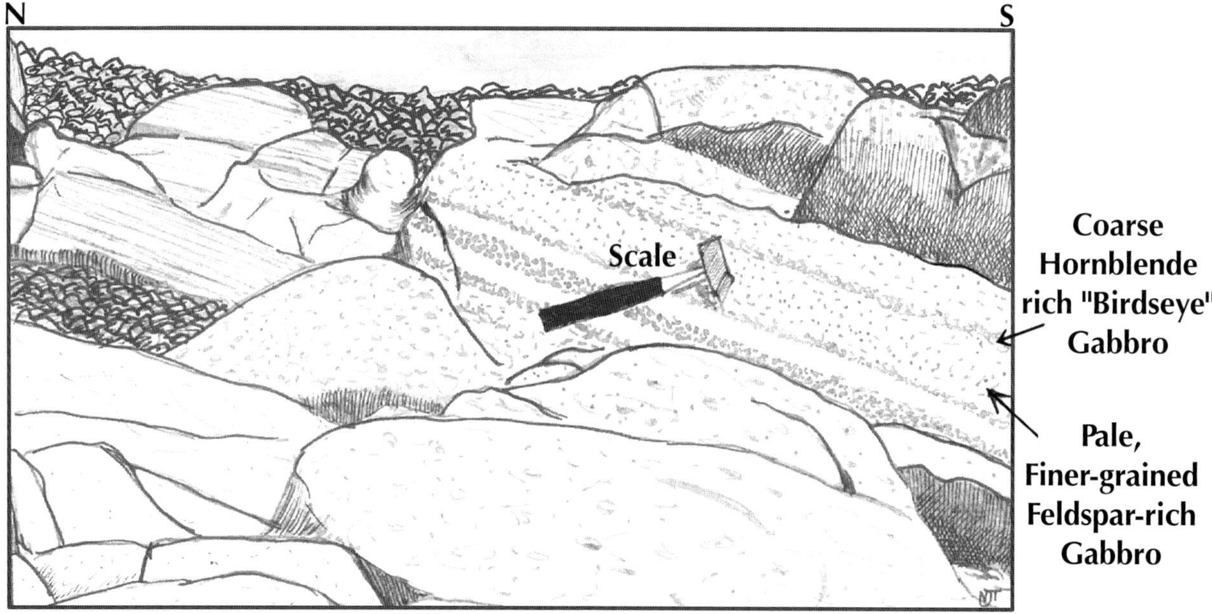

Fig. 15

How can these layers be explained? A recent theory based on evidence from these rocks is now challenging earlier accepted theories of magma crystallisation. This theory suggests that crystallisation first began on the relatively cool floor and walls of the magma chamber. The first crystals of hornblende depleted the surrounding magma of the chemical elements iron and magnesium; thus forming a dark hornblende rich layer. Since the surrounding magma would be depleted in the elements of hornblende, new crystals of lighter coloured feldspar would begin to grow and lay down a feldspar-rich layer. The surrounding magma would then be restored to a more "normal" composition, repeating the process, and thereby developing a succession of light and dark layers. This mechanism can also be used to explain occasional "orbicular" features found here (see Fig 16); these possibly formed around cooler lumps of rock (xenoliths) within the magma.

At the northern end of the bay, beside the Longue Hougue reclamation scheme, is a network of white or pinkish veins. These veins are composed of aplite and also contain angular fragments of dark gabbro. They were formed towards the end of the gabbro crystallisation and represent the final fraction of the feldspar-enriched magma fluid which was forced into fissures under great pressure. As the fluid was squeezed into these fissures, fragments of gabbro broke off and became incorporated into the vein material.

Turn back and walk to the small grassy headland of Spur Point. The gabbro around this headland is composed of black, needle-like crystals of hornblende to the virtual exclusion of other minerals. The rock has a very dark appearance and is a variety of gabbro known as bojite. It is thought that this rock type represents a stage in crystallisation in which the water content of the magma had been increased leading to the rapid growth of these crystals.

On the way back to the car park take a moment to inspect a reef near the high water mark in front of the bunker. Careful examination of this outcrop reveals layers of bojite dipping to the south-east that have been cut by layers of "Bird's Eye" gabbro which lie on top. This relationship suggests that a fresh pulse of magma was injected after the bojite had crystallised, planing off the earlier crystal "mush" before cooling to form a new series of layers.

From the car park take the road through St. Sampson's and past the Vale Castle to the Banque Imbert where the St. Peter Port Gabbro is again well exposed. A stroll along this shoreline will reveal many geological curiosities - rocks which are not native to Guernsey but which have been brought to the island as ballast in ships during the exploitation

Orbicular Structures in St. Peter Port Gabbro.

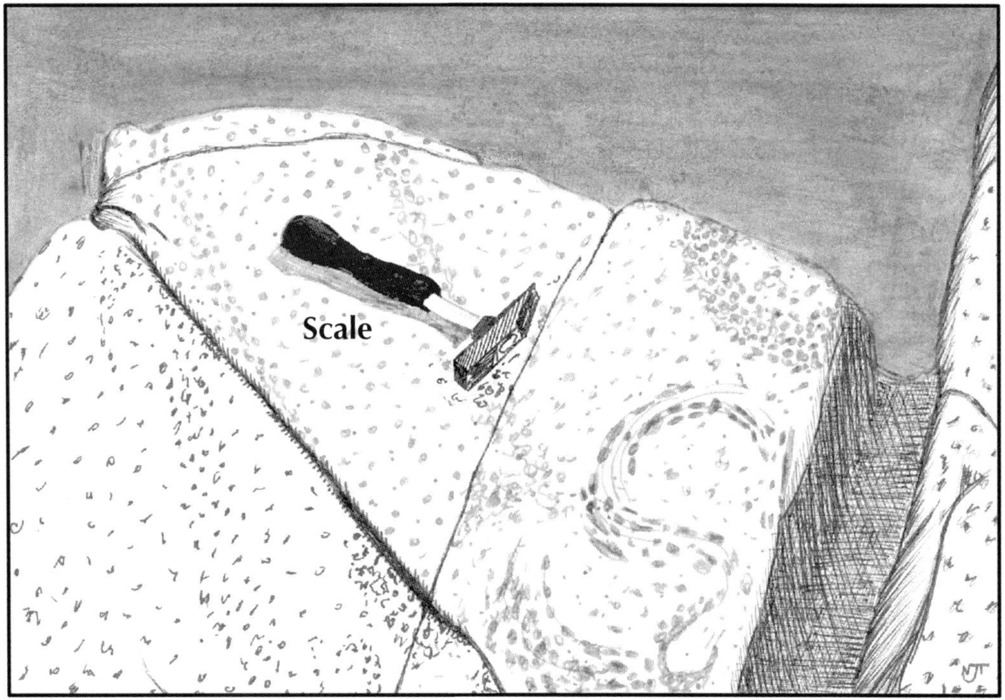

Fig. 16

of the local granite quarries. The variety of rocks includes chalk, flint, limestone, schist and many others, and makes an interesting collecting ground for specimens. On a hot summers day this is also a good place for a swim.

Drive on from this locality to the yacht marina at Beaucette (see St. Sampson-Beaucette map) and make your way around to the southern arm of the marina near the outlet to the sea. The Marina was formerly one of many quarries in the Vale Parish, this industry being the mainstay of Guernsey's economy in the late 19th century. The Bordeaux Diorite is a particularly resistant, massive rock type which could be cut to form quoins, lintels and kerbstones of very high quality, and were hence exported extensively. The quarry was turned into a marina in the 1960's with the help of the Royal Engineers who blasted a gap in the rock wall between the original quarry and the sea.

The diorite here contains some unusual features which have caused considerable debate among geologists. Apparent layering can be seen on the landward side of the arm, similar to that seen in the gabbro, and probably suggesting a similar origin (Fig 17). On the seaward side are some pipe-like structures containing light granitic rock that cut through the diorite at a low angle (Fig 18). They are difficult to explain but it is thought that they relate to the mixing of two immiscible magma bodies, one of dark, diorite composition and the other of pale granite composition. One idea about their origin is that the lower density granite melt might have risen through the diorite melt as a series of "blobs", stretched out into low-angle "pipes" as a result of slow horizontal flow in the diorite. Much work has yet to be done before a satisfactory explanation can be made, and the reader's own ideas may well provide as good an explanation as any other!

Layered Bordeaux Diorite, Beaucette Marina.

Fig. 17

Granite Pipes, Beaucette Marina

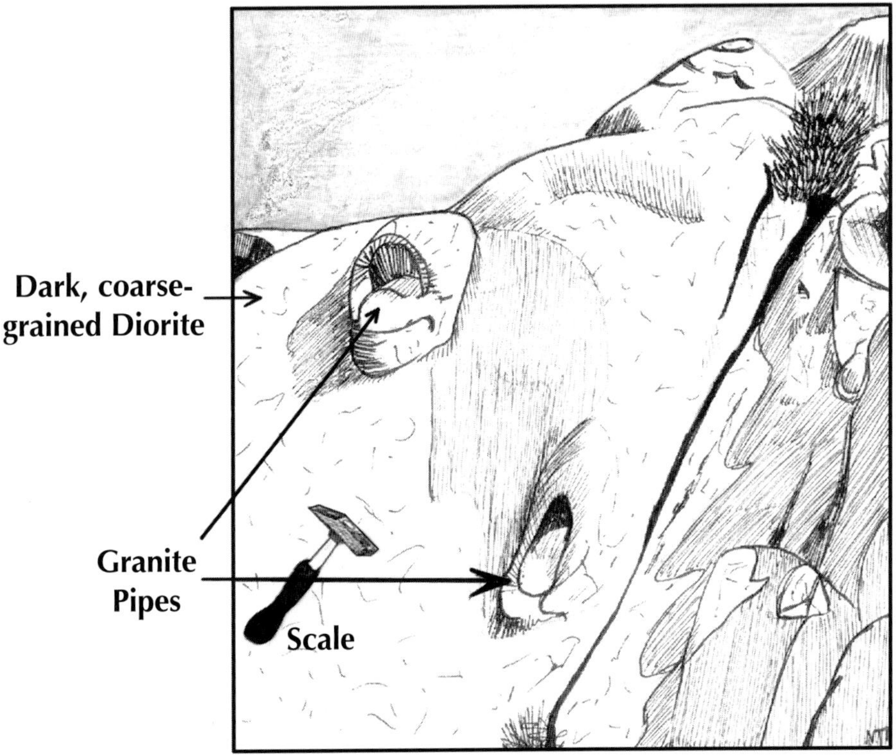

Fig. 18

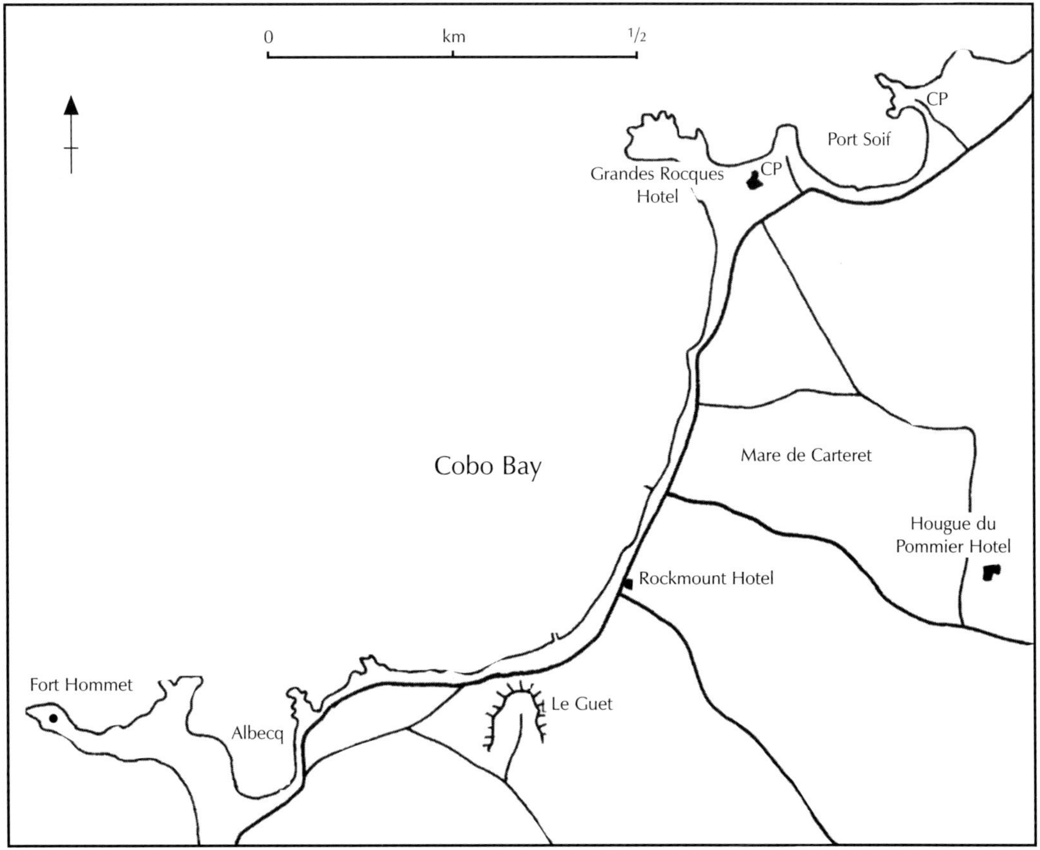

Itinerary 6

Cobo Bay - Port Soif

ITINERARY 6 - COBO, ALBECQ AND PORT SOIF

Cobo is one of the island's most popular and picturesque bays, both for its sandy beach and excellent windsurfing. Dominating the southern side of the bay is Le Guet, a wooded hill topped by a small gun battery and signalling station dating from Napoleonic times. The side of this hill was quarried in the nineteenth century, the orangey-pink coloured Cobo granite of the quarry face being instantly recognisable as the source of much local building stone as well as the stone used in several buildings in St. Peter Port such as the Market (see Itinerary 7). A number of smaller disused quarries are also found in the area.

A glance at the geological map on the back cover of this book reveals that both the Cobo Granite and the Bordeaux Diorite outcrop in this bay. The contact between these two rock types can be seen in the centre of the bay and also at Port Soif, further to the north. This contact, however, is far from simple. Both rocks appear to contain inclusions of the other type in a contact zone that is quite wide. Recent research suggests the possibility that the two rock types may be of very similar age, and the different magmas mixed where they met together.

Start immediately to the west of the Rockmount Hotel where a small outcrop of rock occurs on the beach approximately 30 metres from the sea wall. These rocks are somewhat greyer than those that make up the scenic Cobo/Albecq headland where the pink Cobo Granite has been sculptured by the sea to produce the panorama shown in Fig 19. The reason for the difference in colour is due to the mixing of two different magmas as mentioned above. It appears that the grey Bordeaux Diorite had virtually crystallised but was still in a "plastic" state when the Cobo Granite was intruded. The two bodies, therefore, mixed together and produced a hybrid rock - a combination of both granite and diorite. Apart from the greyish colour, this outcrop does not display other features produced by mixing particularly well.

Walk across the beach in a direct line towards the slipway to the south of Cobo below Le Guet. As the sandy beach gives way to a low rock platform, look for darker patches of rock within the pink granite. Here the distinction between the two rock types is better seen and the evidence of magma mixing is well displayed. Sometimes dark grey angular xenoliths of diorite can be found enclosed by the granite indicating that the diorite must have pre-dated the granite and must have already been crystallised. Perhaps the heat of the granite then partially re-melted the diorite to produce other features seen here where the granite and the hybrid rock appear to be mixed together. Walk a little way across this rock platform towards Albecq and it will be seen that the Cobo Granite becomes steadily purer with fewer and fewer inclusions the further one goes. The granite itself is coarse grained and composed predominantly of feldspar and quartz. The pink colour is due to the potassium-rich orthoclase feldspar, the other type of feldspar (plagioclase) present is light grey. The quartz grains are glassy in appearance, whilst the small black shiny crystals present are of biotite mica. If desired, the granite can be further examined at Albecq, whilst the granite-diorite contact is well exposed at low tide in Port Soif.

To reach Albecq, take the footpath along the main road from the slipway towards the headland passing the quarry at Le Guet on the left. As the road makes the bend on the headland towards Albecq Bay, take the small rough path out onto the rocky headland. Vertical drill holes in the nearby rocks testify to more recent quarrying activity, possibly by the occupying German forces between 1940-1945. Here, however, the granite is superbly exposed due to the fresh surfaces from the quarrying. The path disappears on the headland and from there clamber down over the rocks to the west into a small cove which leads back towards the road. At the back of the cove is a small exposure of 8m raised beach which is overlain by angular head deposit. On the west side of the cove is a narrow gully about 1m wide containing a greenish-looking rock extending in an east-west direction. This is a lamprophyre dyke - the hydrous ferromagnesian minerals of which it is composed are unstable under atmospheric conditions and are easily eroded by the sea leaving a gully within the granite.

Hommet headland, on the west side of Albecq, has further good exposures of the Cobo Granite; the fortifications here (dating from 16th Century to World War II) are also well worth visiting.

Port Soif lies in the opposite direction, to the N E of Cobo, and can be reached on foot or by means of a short drive. It is at its prettiest at high water, with the sea completely filling the horseshoe-shaped bay, guarded by its narrow northern entrance. The reason for its shape is best ascertained at low tide, however, when it is possible to walk across the bay mouth and examine the rock exposure in the foreshore.

Examination of the rocks of the headlands to the west and east of the bay mouth reveal them to be made up of pink Cobo Granite and greyish Bordeaux Diorite respectively, with "marginal" rocks (like those at Cobo) comprising the intervening foreshore. These rocks between the headlands are also quite heavily jointed. It is this feature which has allowed the sea to pick out the weakened rock and begin to erode the bay beyond. The jointing itself may result from stresses set up by slow movement of the viscous magmas relative to each other as they crystallized - stresses which caused the rock to crack and weaken many millions of years later and hence allowed the bay to form.

Le Guet, Cobo

Fig. 19

Foreshore composed of pink Cobo Granite showing horizontal and vertical joints and containing occasional xenoliths.

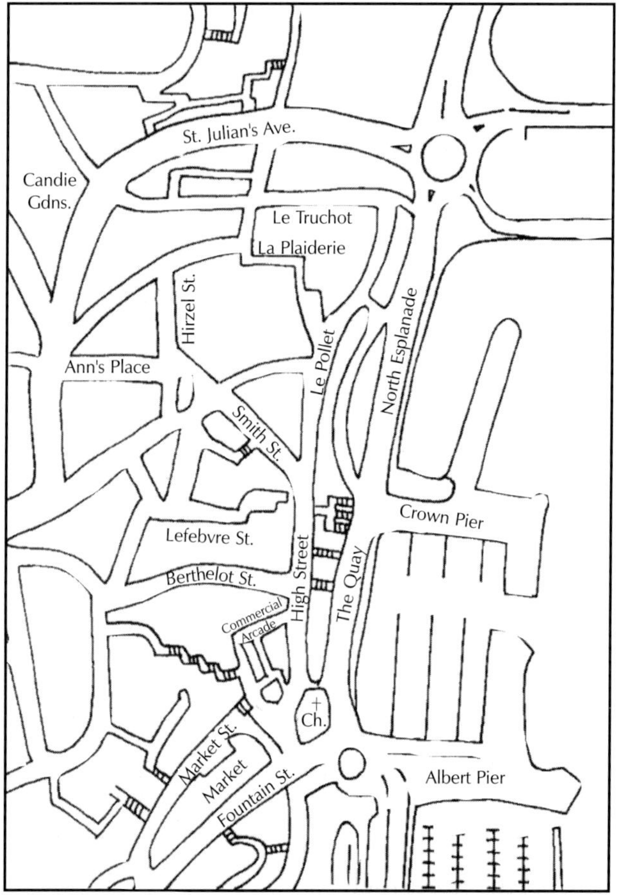

Itinerary 7

St. Peter Port

ITINERARY 7 - ST. PETER PORT TOWN CENTRE

Town centres are always of interest to the geologist as they often provide the chance to examine a wider variety of rocks in a small area than can ever be found in nature. St. Peter Port is no exception. This short "geological trail" (takes about an hour) begins, appropriately, at the Town Church, which is itself built of a wide variety of both local and imported stone.

The rough stonework of the church's exterior is made up of a very wide variety of rock types, many of which (to judge by their rounded appearance) were simply picked up off the beach by the builders. In the region of the plaque dedicated to Major General Sir Isaac Brock, immediately to the left of the porch, the authors found examples of virtually every Guernsey rock type as well as rough-hewn blocks of imported granite and limestone (a piece of the latter contains many shells of water-snails, possibly from the Purbeck beds of Dorset).

The fifteenth century porch of the church is built of skillfully dressed and carved granite from the Chausey Islands, south of Jersey. The large quarries there begun by the Benedictine monks who built the Mont St. Michel, exported a great deal of stone, which may be found in several of Guernsey's churches and older Town buildings. The same stone was also used for the arches and columns of the church interior and for the gable-end wall facing the Market. The porch and church interior are floored with limestone flags which came from the Portland Stone quarries on the Dorset coast, whilst the tracery of many of the vaulted windows in the Church are carved from the white Caen limestone. Also inside the church, the font, pulpit and many wall plaques are carved from a variety of types of marble, probably of French or Italian origin.

From the church walk up to the Market building (Les Halles). A marvellous piece of mid-nineteenth century architecture, built with funds raised by the simple expedient of printing extra money, it is built of dressed Herm 'granite' quoins and columns and Cobo granite blocks. The Guille-Allez Library, close by, also has a fine entrance porch of Herm granodiorite with polished columns of a pink granite, probably from Aberdeen.

From the Market Square, descend the steps and walk through the Commercial Arcade to the High Street. Immediately, there are a host of different rock types to be seen in buildings and shop fronts, and in the cobbles and kerbs of the street itself.

The modern facings of Woolworth's and Creasey's shops are made from a polished diorite of foreign origin, the kerbstones are of Herm Granodiorite and the cobbles of a mixture of local gabbro, granodiorite and diorite.

Turn left up the High Street. The T.S.B. Bank is housed in an old building on the corner of Berthelot Street built of Chausey Granite. A short walk up this street reveals another old house on the left whose main building material is a coarse sandstone from Alderney. Looking back down to the High Street, the building which faces you (part of Creasey's) is built of a rather inferior granite from Normandy, containing patches of iron-rich minerals which have weathered out as rather unsightly black spots.

Return to the High Street. The entrance to the next shop up the hill from Creasey's is faced with a greenish-grey banded stone. This is a volcanic rock from the English Lake District known as tuff. The rock is actually made up of layers of volcanic "ash" - each representing an eruption, although in this case the layers have been laid in water and re-worked by currents. The same rock type has also been used on other shop fronts in the High Street and the Pollet.

Further up the High Street, the National Westminster Bank is again built of Herm stone, the "Old Bank" building has polished pink granite pillars similar to those of the Library mentioned previously. Beyond this, a variety of rocks are used in shop doorways, including a brecciated limestone veined with greeny-yellow epidote, pale green veined marble and, on the opposite side of the street, dark Norwegian Larvikite, with its characteristic shimmering crystals of feldspar.

Where the High Street branches into Smith Street and the Pollet, the Lloyds Bank building shows an attractive combination of dressed Chausey Granite and Guernsey Diorite.

Continue down the Pollet. Rocks such as marble, larvikite, and volcanic tuff may be recognised in several of the shop fronts along this street.

Moore's Hotel, made up largely of dressed Herm granodiorite and Guernsey diorite, is at another fork in the road. Take the left fork and follow the "pedestrianised" lane known as La Plaiderie (an old wall on the left contains a variety of rocks including limestone from Devon as well as local types). The new finance offices here are faced with French granites (the cobbles are also of this material) and English brick.

The next road left, Hospital Lane, is worth a glance up to the old St. Peter Port Hospital (now the Police Headquarters). Built of dark grey Guernsey diorite and gabbro, it has, however, a fine entrance gateway built of pink Jersey granite.

Continue to the main road, St. Julian's Avenue. From here, a short walk up the hill beneath the retaining walls built of St. Peter Port Gabbro, brings you to Candie Gardens and the Museum, which has a good display on local geology and archaeology. Alternatively, walk down hill past the office buildings (faced with a variety of mainly French granites and, in one case, sandstone) to the sea front. From here, it is a short walk back along the front (or through the Pollet) to the church. The route along the sea front also gives the opportunity to further examine the variety of mainly local stone used in the construction of the harbour and harbour front buildings.

HERM

Pointe du Gentilhomme
Shell Beach
Belvoir Bay
Puffin Bay
Farm
Café
Toilets
Café
Pierre des Rats (Obelisk)
Le Manoir
Le Creux Pigeon
Fisherman's Cottage
Mouisonniere Beach
Quarry
Dolmen
The Common
White House
Hotel
Quarries
Rosaire Cottage
Old Mine Shaft
Pt. Sauzebourge
Le Petit Monceau
Fishermans Beach
Cemetery
Harbour
Rosaire Steps
Oyster Point
Hermetier
Le Plat Houmet
Percée

ITINERARY 8 - HERM

Seen from Guernsey, the flat plateau of Herm and its sister island, Jethou, show clearly one of the late Tertiary wave-cut platform levels (at around 60m) referred to in the Introduction Fig 20, (The Sark plateau beyond is at a higher, 90m level). Herm is divided into two parts, the southern rock plateau just referred to, and the low-lying sand dunes which form the northern part of the island. An examination of depth contours on the Admiralty Chart suggests that the Little Russell (stretch of sea dividing Herm and Jethou from Guernsey) marks the head of a drowned southward-flowing river valley cut during the "glacial periods" of the last half-million years when sea-level was much lower than it is now.

A walk around Herm is easily accomplished in a couple of hours and includes a number of features of geological interest.

Starting from the harbour, it is worth walking northward along the western shore for about 100m or so, to view the boulders near the top of the beach below the lower camping field. These are composed of typical Herm Granodiorite, a coarse-grained grey igneous rock, similar to the paler varieties of Guernsey's Bordeaux Diorite complex and composed largely of feldspar and quartz with biotite and hornblende. Of particular interest, however, is the frequent occurrence of dark lumps (or xenoliths) within the granodiorite which must be the remains of an earlier rock type, perhaps gabbro, into which the Herm granodiorite intruded, or, perhaps, evidence of co-existing magmas (see Itineraries 5 and 6)

Herm harbour, originally more extensive than today, was constructed to serve the quarries that can still be seen along the island's west coast. The largest of these was quite deep, though is now largely infilled by rubbish. The remains of an old crane for loading stone still occupies the harbour jetty. Quarrying began in 1815 and by the middle of the nineteenth century, employed around 400 people.

As in Guernsey, the stone was cut in blocks from the face by first drilling a line of holes (usually about 20cm deep and a similar distance apart) using a hammer and "jumper" - the latter being a sort of long cold-chisel held and turned by one labourer, whilst another hit it with a heavy sledge hammer ... the result of a mis-hit often being a serious injury! Wedges were then driven into the holes so as to crack the rock apart along the required line. Finally, the blocks were

Herm and Jethou (from St. Sampson)

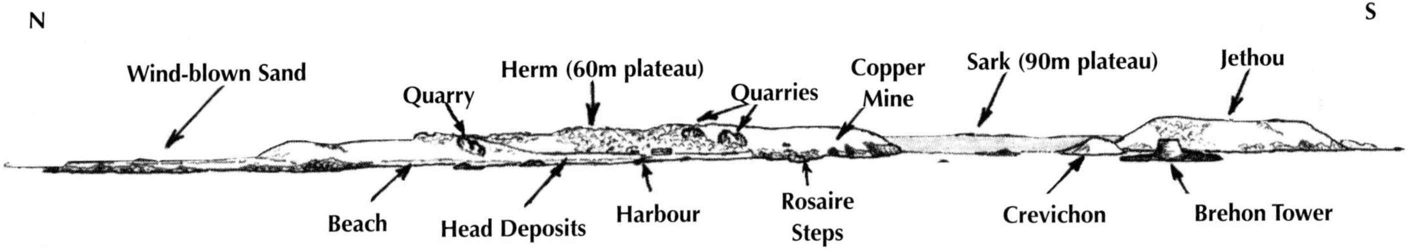

Fig. 20

further cut and dressed as required using stone hammers. Stone was exported mainly to England for use as kerbstones also for use in the Thames embankment and other projects. Tests carried out in London showed "Herm Granite" to be the most durable of rocks, outlasting English and Scottish granites in resisting the abrasion and impact of metal-rimmed carriage and cartwheels. Herm granite was also used in the construction of the St. Peter Port Halles (Market building), its dark xenoliths being easily recognised in this building. By the 1860's however, the competition from the larger and more efficient Guernsey quarries, led to the decline and demise of the Herm industry. Further details on the stone industry are given in the exhibitions at the Guernsey Museum in Candie Gardens, or the Folk Museum at Saumarez Park.

From the harbour, follow the path south towards Rosaire Steps and branch left along the cliff path around the south end of the island. A little way up this path can still be seen a block of stone left by the quarrymen containing holes which were drilled as outlined previously.

Towards the southern tip of the island (about 200m south of Rosaire Steps), a large fenced-off gorse bush on the left-hand side of the path masks the top of a small mine shaft; overgrown remains of a small spoil tip may also be discerned lower down the slope. Lead and copper mining on Herm began in 1837, following the discovery of silver (and lead) ore on Little Sark in 1833. Whilst the Sark mine enjoyed some early success (see "The Rocks of Sark" by Wes Gibbons), the thin veins of lead and copper ore found in Herm rapidly proved too small to be economically viable, and the venture was abandoned within a year or so.

The path around the south-eastern part of the island provides spectacular views of the rugged cliffs and across the Great Russell to Sark. The cliffs of this part of the island are cut by several faults, weaknesses which have been exploited by the sea to form deep gullies and sea caves, such as Barbara's Leap and Le Creux Pigeon. The crumbling rock and sandy soils towards the cliff tops hereabouts provide nesting sites for the small puffin colony which regularly breeds on Herm.

Belvoir Bay provides a pleasant refreshment stop, as well as an opportunity to further examine the Herm granodiorite. As in many Guernsey bays, the cliffs at Belvoir are partly composed of head deposits (similar to those described, for example at Moulin Huet) formed during the last glaciation.

The beach sands of Belvoir Bay and Shell Beach further to the north are well worth examining. They are formed largely of shell material (including many intact shells of various molluscs) swept together by the combined action of tidal currents and waves, and provide a good illustration of how some types of shelly limestones may have accumulated in the past.

The dunes of northern Herm are made up largely of blown shell sand, deposited on top of the remains of the extensive "fossil" wave-cut platform which extends to the north of the island as a series of treacherous reefs. The blown sand deposits have buried evidence of early settlement of the island - the observant walker will quite easily find the remains of a buried dolmen (passage grave) on the western side of the island 100m or so north-east of the cemetery. The slow accumulation of sand which has enlarged the island considerably over the last few thousand years, is now threatened by tourist traffic which has damaged the grass cover in many places - man, too, can be an important (if inadvertent) agent in geological processes.

Also at the northern end of Herm, a stone obelisk, used as a navigation marker, now stands where there was formerly a Neolithic standing stone (dolmen), removed last century by quarrymen.

A short distance to the east, there is a prominent rock outcrop on the beach, which can be examined even at fairly high tide. The outcrop is composed of typical Herm granodiorite, except that it is particularly rich in the characteristic dark xenoliths mentioned previously, especially on its eastern side (see Fig 21). However, the xenoliths here show an interesting variation in appearance, which has sparked off recent discussion amongst local geologists.

Their nature varies from dark, angular pieces of diorite through to much paler coloured, more rounded 'blobs', sometimes outlined by a faint rim of darker minerals. On the eastern side of the outcrop, a slab of rock seems to be composed entirely of these dark lumps, veined through with more granitic material. Their origin can only be speculated on, but it is possible that they originally formed a larger 'blob' of semi-consolidated diorite which was surrounded by the granodiorite melt.

Either the diorite began to break up and become absorbed by the paler magma (unlikely, since the paler rock probably would have had a lower melting point) or else hot fluids, escaping under pressure from within the granodiorite body as it crystallised and cooled, cracked apart the diorite mass and gradually altered its composition. Similar hot fluids (consisting of water, carbon dioxide and other volatiles) are also thought to form veins of aplite and pegmatite, and may have caused the recrystallisation of feldspar megacrysts in the L'Eree granite.

The degree to which xenoliths have been altered or 'absorbed' into the granodiorite may depend on the extent to which they were affected by these high pressure fluids. The 'mineral veins' around some xenoliths seem to support this theory.

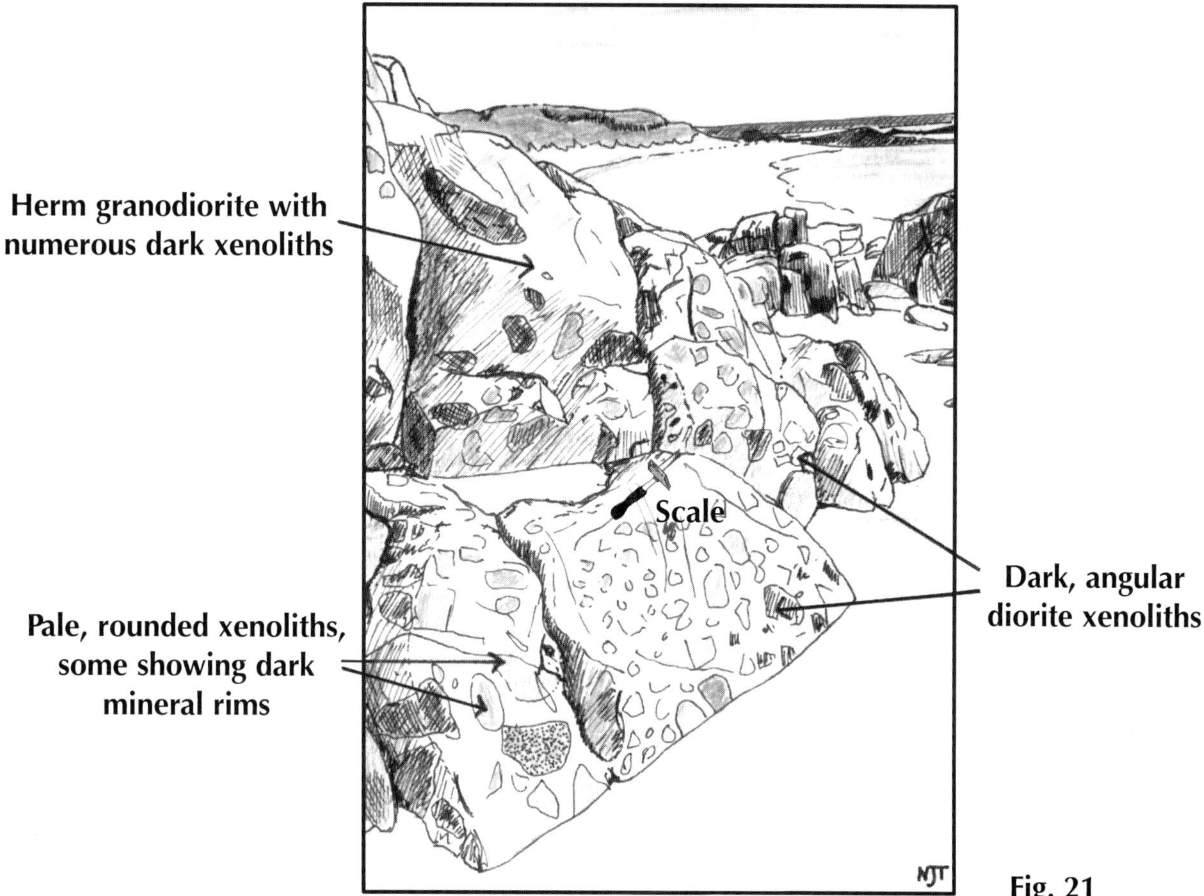
Herm granodiorite with numerous dark xenoliths
Scale
Dark, angular diorite xenoliths
Pale, rounded xenoliths, some showing dark mineral rims
NJT

Fig. 21

BIBLIOGRAPHY

1. British Geological Survey. Geological Map (Solid and Drift) of Guernsey with accompanying notes. A very useful and pretty publication!
2. R. A. Roach: "Outline and Guide to the Geology of Guernsey". Extract from "*Transactions of La Société Guernesiaise*" Vol.XVII. A fairly short but technical Guide, comprising nine detailed geological itineraries.
3. Roach, Topley, Brown et al: "*Outline and Guide to the Geology of Guernsey*". Museum Monograph Series, Candie Museum. A much extended and updated version of Dr. Roach's original guide.
4. J. T. Renouf: Geology. In Coysh, V. (Ed) "*The Channel Islands: A New Study*" (David & Charles) A clear and readable account of the geological evolution of the Channel Islands.
5. Nigel Jee: "*Landscape of the Channel Islands*" (Phillimore). An extensive account of the evolution, both natural and man-made of the Channel Islands' landscape.
6. Wes Gibbons: "*The Rocks of Sark*". Visitors to Sark are recommended to obtain this excellent booklet.

Many of the above include extensive lists of references to numerous articles in the Transactions of La Société Guernesiaise and other publications.

APPENDIX

Some Fundamentals of Geology

Geology is, essentially, the study of rocks, the minerals of which they are made, the fossils which they contain and the Earth processes which form them and shape the landscape.

MINERALS are the naturally-occurring chemical substances, usually crystals, which make up all rocks. Most common rock forming minerals are silicates, i.e. compounds of various elements with silicon and oxygen. The most common minerals found in Guernsey's rocks are Quartz, Feldspar, Mica and Hornblende (see Glossary), though many other minerals are also found.

ROCKS are made up of grains or crystals of minerals (such as quartz); they can be divided into three classes:

Igneous rocks are formed when the rock deep beneath the Earth's surface melts to form magma. This molten material then rises either to erupt as lava from volcanoes or to cool and crystallise within the Earth's crust in the form of igneous intrusions.

The rocks which form the northern half of Guernsey are largely intrusive igneous rocks, such as Granite, Diorite, Gabbro and Dolerite (see Glossary). Originally intruded into the crust thousands of metres below the surface, they have been exposed after millions of years of slow uplift and erosion.

Sedimentary rocks are formed by the deposition of mud, sand grains, pebbles, etc. by water, wind or ice. These sediments are slowly compressed by the overlying layers and cemented by mineral material deposited from ground water. Guernsey has little in the way of sedimentary rocks, but some of its oldest rocks are of sedimentary origin (the Pleinmont and Jerbourg metasediments).

Metamorphic rocks are rocks which have been greatly altered by the action of heat and pressure resulting from Earth movements or igneous intrusion. Like igneous rocks, metamorphic rocks are crystalline, but typically show a parallel alignment of minerals. Typical examples found in Guernsey are gneisses, such as the Icart Gneiss; and schists, such as the Jerbourg metasediment (see Glossary). Also formed deep within the Earth's crust, these rocks are now exposed after millions of years of uplift and erosion.

GEOLOGICAL TIME. The processes which form rocks take place over very long time periods - of the order of millions of years. Until comparatively recently, however, it was impossible to determine the age of a rock in millions of years. The advent of a technique called radiometric dating now enables geologists to date rocks of igneous or metamorphic origin with reasonable certainty, and we now know that the rocks of southern Guernsey are some of the oldest in Europe, around 2,500 million years old. An explanation of radiometric dating techniques is beyond the scope of this booklet, but essentially it relies on the development of technology to accurately measure trace amounts of naturally-occurring radioactive elements (whose radioactive decay rates are known) in rock samples. Radiometric dates accord well with other evidence for the relative order of formation of rocks and fossils, long-established in a form known as the Geological Column,as given at the end of this appendix.

PLATE TECTONICS. Geologists have long known that the Earth's crust is by no means stable or static and, where one part of the crust moves against another, huge forces may build up, slowly bending rocks into folds or breaking them along faults - the source of earthquakes. At such sites of stress within the crust, magma may form and give rise to igneous activity.

In recent years, a pattern of such activity has become widely recognised and forms the basis of the theory of Plate Tectonics. According to this theory the Earth's outer layer is made up of a series of rigid "plates" which are in a state of slow - but almost irresistible - motion in relation to each other, and to the hot, slightly plastic, mantle layer beneath. The mechanisms which cause this motion are complex, and still a matter of debate.

In some regions, such as in the Atlantic Ocean, plates are moving apart (measurements show the Atlantic is widening at a rate of up to 4cm per year); the result of this motion is the formation of new ocean-floor crust by underwater volcanic eruptions at the mid-ocean ridge (see below). The rocks of the ocean crust are destroyed (or re-absorbed) in other areas where the plates are moving together. Such sites are known as subduction zones, and are often regions of intense crustal compression, earthquakes and volcanic activity, such as present-day western South America or Japan. It is principally where plates collide that mountain-building (Orogeny) takes place as the crust becomes compressed and uplifted, and rocks are deformed and metamorphosed. The diagram overleaf summarises the main types of plate boundaries although, in practice, an almost infinite variety of geological situations are possible. (For further reading, see Bibliography).

Summary Section to show main types of plate boundary

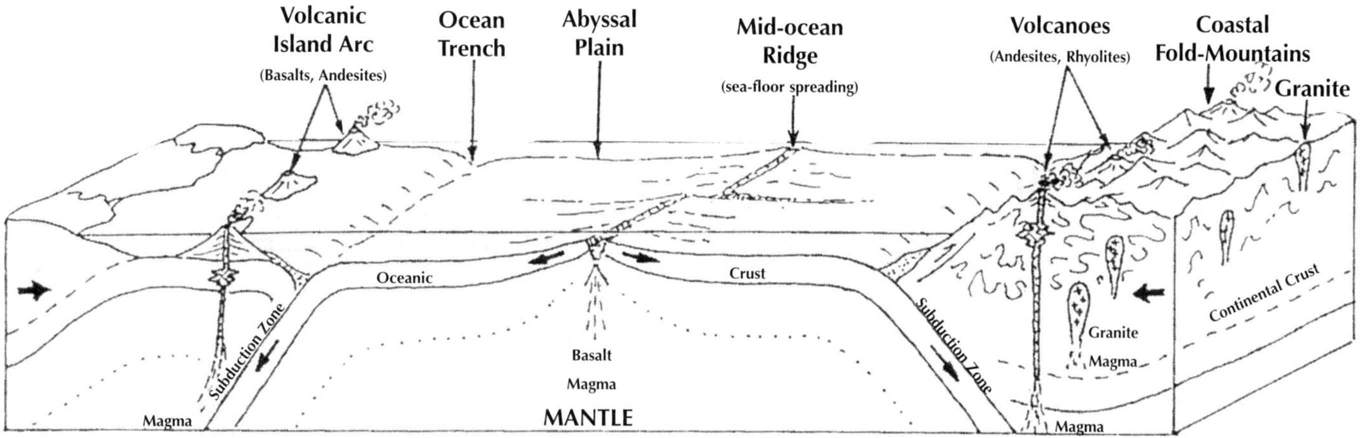

The Cadomian Orogeny, which affected north-west France and the Channel Islands some 500 million years ago, involved the subduction of ocean crust to the north-west of Guernsey beneath a continental margin that lay to the south-east. The volcanic rocks of Jersey and the igneous intrusions of northern Guernsey resulted from magma generated by partial melting in the subduction zone beneath a newly-forming range of coastal fold-mountains, of which the islands today represent a last fragment.

The erosion of these mountains by rivers during the Palaeozoic Era led, in turn, to the formation of the red Rozel Conglomerate in Jersey, the Alderney Sandstone, and similar rocks in the Cotentin Peninsula.

Age (my)	Era	Period	Major Events	Local Events & Rock Types
0	Quarternary	Pleistocene	Glaciations	Head & Raised Beach deposits
2	Tertiary	Neogene		High Sea levels - Plateaux
		Palaeogene	Atlantic opening	
65	Mesozoic	Cretaceous Jurassic Triassic }	Age of the Dinosaurs	Chalk Sea around C.I.
225		}	Britain a desert	
	Palaeozoic	Permian }		
			Variscan Orogeny	∧∧∧ Lamprophyre dykes (295 my)
		Carboniferous	Coal Swamps	
		Devonian	First fish/plants Caledonian Orogy	
		Silurian		
		Ordovician	Sea covers most of Britain	
		Cambrian	Earliest Fossils	Formation of N. Igneous complex in Guernsey: 500-650 my
570				∧∧∧ Cadomian Orogeny
	Proterozoic	(Brioverian)	———	Pleinmont Metasediment
		(Pentevrian)	———	Formation of southern Metamorphic complex in Guernsey: 1000-2500 my
3500	Archaean	No record in Europe		
4600		Formation of Earth		

∧∧∧ = Period of deformation and mountain-building.

Glossary of Geological Terms

Aplite	A pale pinkish or brownish fine-grained rock which commonly occurs in small veins cutting through granites, diorites, etc.
Armorica	Name for the region of the Earth's crust comprising Brittany, Cotentin and the Channel Islands.
Augite	A dark green or black mineral common in igneous rocks such as gabbro and basalt.
Biotite	See Mica
Brioverian	Period of Pre-Cambrian time, from about 1000 to 700 million years ago.
Cadomian	A mountain-building period (Orogeny), around 450-600 million years ago, during which the igneous rocks of northern Guernsey were formed.
Chalk	Soft, white limestone formed during the Cretaceous Period (the rock which forms the white cliffs of Dover).
Diorite	A coarse-grained greyish igneous rock, made up largely of the two minerals feldspar and hornblende. The Bordeaux Diorite forms part of northern Guernsey. (see Geological Map)
Dip	Orientation (slope and direction) of a rock surface or layer.
Dolerite	A dark grey, medium-grained igneous rock, commonly forming dykes. Similar composition to basalt and gabbro.
Dyke	Sheet-like igneous intrusion, commonly of dolerite, and usually a few metres thick. Formed by intrusion of magma along cracks or faults in the crust. See Itinerary 1, Fig.5.
Epidote	A yellowish-green mineral commonly found in cracks and faults.
Erosion	The process of wearing away rocks by the action of wind, water or ice.

Fault — A crack in the Earth's crust along which one portion of rock has moved against another. Faults often contain broken-up rock (fault breccias) and are usually zones of weakness picked out by wave erosion to form gullies and sea caves.

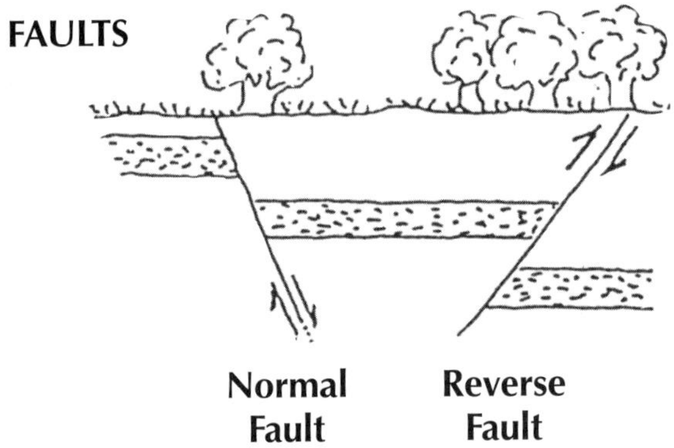

Feldspar — A white, pinkish, brownish or colourless mineral, commonly forming rectangular crystals and often showing flat, cleaved surfaces which glint in the sun. Feldspar is a constituent of almost all igneous rocks, but is typically best seen in granites such as at L'Erée. Conspicuous pinkish feldspar crystals are also a feature of the Icart Gneiss.

Flint — Nodules of hard, microcrystalline silica formed in the Chalk and found on Guernsey beaches.

Fold — Bending of rock layers due to compression of the Earth's crust.

Fossil — Any trace of past life found in rocks. In Guernsey, the only fossils likely to be found are occasional remains of sponges and sea-urchins preserved in flint pebbles washed up on beaches.

Gabbro	A coarse-grained igneous rock, dark grey in colour (sometimes almost black) made up largely of feldspar, hornblende and augite. Sometimes shows alternating layers of minerals - see Itinerary 5 (St. Peter Port Gabbro).
Glaciation	During the last 500,000 years or so, the climate has, for several periods, become much cooler than at present, causing ice sheets to cover much of Britain. Though these ice sheets did not reach as far south as the Channel Islands, Guernsey experienced arctic tundra conditions at these times. Three main glaciations are recognised, known as the Anglian, Wolstonian and Devensian separated by the Hoxnian and Ipswichian "Interglacials" respectively. The retreat of the last (Devensian) glaciation took place about 10,000 years ago. During interglacial periods, climate was similar to the present day - at times warmer.
Gneiss	A coarse-grained, crystalline metamorphic rock, often banded in appearance or showing an alignment of minerals such as feldspar, as in the Icart and Perelle gneisses of Guernsey.
Granite	A pale grey or pinkish, coarse-grained igneous rock made up of Feldspar, Quartz, Mica and sometimes Hornblende. There are two examples of this rock type in Guernsey, the L'Erée and Cobo granites.
Granodiorite	Another coarse-grained igneous rock, intermediate in composition between Granite and Diorite. Examples are L'Ancresse and Herm Granodiorites.
Head	A sedimentary deposit made up of angular rock fragments embedded in finer-grained sand and silt, seen at several places around Guernsey's coast (e.g. Moulin Huet). It was formed during glacial periods when frozen ground, containing ice-shattered rock, melted and slumped downhill during the warmer months.
Hornblende	A black mineral which is an important constituent of rocks such as diorite, and the main dark-coloured mineral in the St. Peter Port Gabbro. A noticeable mineral in the rocks of old walls in Town, often glinting in sunlight.

Ice Age	See Glaciation.
Inclusion	Small crystals of one mineral found within larger crystals of another (or sometimes small xenoliths within a rock).
Interglacial	See Glaciation.
Lamprophyre	A medium-grained igneous rock, brown in colour and often quite rich in mica; intruded as dykes during the Variscan Orogeny.
Loess	Deposits of yellowish windblown dust, derived from the glacial outwash regions of northern Europe. Loess forms the basis of much of Guernsey's soil.
Megacryst	Unusually large crystal e.g. Feldspar crystals in the L'Eree granite.
Mica	A soft, shiny, flaky mineral, common in granites and some metamorphic rocks such as schist and gneiss. Two common varieties are black biotite and pale brown muscovite.
Muscovite	See Mica.
Olivine	Green mineral found in some igneous rocks such as gabbro.
Orogeny	A mountain-building period - see also Appendix.
Pegamite	A very coarse grained rock, composed usually of feldspar, quartz, mica or hornblende, often forming pods or veins in granites, etc.
Pentevrian	A substantial period of Pre-Cambrian time, from about 2500 million years to 1000 million years ago during which the Icart and Perelle gneisses formed.
Quartz	A colourless, white or greyish glassy-looking mineral, an important constituent of granites and granodiorites, sandstones, schists and gneisses. In addition, quartz commonly occurs as a vein mineral - seen especially at Marble Bay.

Raised Beach	A sedimentary deposit made up of rounded pebbles and sand, seen in several places around Guernsey's coast. Raised Beaches were formed during Interglacial periods when sea level was higher than at present.
Schist	A medium-grained metamorphic rock, often thinly layered (foliated) and rich in Mica. The Jerbourg Metasediment includes some rather poor examples.
Shale	A sedimentary rock formed from compressed mud.
Tectonic	A term referring to the formation of folds and faults by stresses within the Earth's crust.
Variscan	A mountain-building episode (Orogeny) which occurred about 300 million years ago, in which Armorica and Britain became joined. Lamprophyre dykes intruded in Guernsey.
Vein	A thin, sheetlike body of Aplite, Pegmatite or minerals such as Quartz, formed by deposition of minerals from hot fluids escaping upward through the crust, along faults or other fractures.
Wave-cut notch	A notch cut at the base of a cliff by wave action.
Wave-cut platform	A rock platform, cut at around low tide level, by prolonged wave action over several thousand years.
Weathering	The process of breaking down rocks exposed at the surface through the chemical or physical action of the weather.
Xenolith	A lump of the surrounding rock which becomes engulfed by an intruding magma, typically seen as dark lumps within granites/granodiorites such as at L'Erée or in Herm.

Notes: